HEALTHY COOKING

HEALTHY COOKING

The Best, the Healthiest Recipes Selected from Cuisines around the World

by

Sharon Claessens

Edited by Carol Keough

 Rodale Press, Emmaus, Pennsylvania

Printed in the United States of America on recycled paper containing a high percentage of de-inked fiber.

Art Director: Jerry O'Brien
Designers: Lynn Foulk, Alison Lee

**Library of Congress Cataloging
in Publication Data**

Claessens, Sharon.
    Healthy cooking.

    (The Prevention total health system)
    Includes index.
    1. Cookery (Natural foods)   I. Title.
II. Series.
TX741.C575   1985   641.5′63   84-8251
ISBN 0-87857-559-6 paperback

2   4   6   8   10   9   7   5   3   1   paperback

Notice

This book is intended as a reference volume only, not as a medical manual or guide to self-treatment. Keep in mind that nutritional and health needs vary from person to person, depending on age, sex, health status and total diet. The information here is intended to help you make informed decisions about your diet, but is not to be used as a substitute for any treatment that may have been prescribed by your doctor.

Contents

Preface

Good Eating and Good Health

It was barely a generation ago that indigestion, heartburn and ulcers were considered the very signs of "success." Even alcohol abuse was considered part of the "successful lifestyle" in business or the arts—providing, of course, that one drank only luxury brands. Food was essentially irrelevant to any notion of success, so long as the gin was cold, the beef was hot, and there was plenty of both.

What a distance we've traveled since then!

What is our notion of success today?

A recent Gallup Poll revealed the astonishing fact that people now equate success not with a wonderful job, not with a beautiful home, not, in fact, with any traditional measure of accomplishment. Rather, the poll—commissioned by *Success* magazine—found the current notion of success is *good health*.

And why not?

With health, and all that the word now implies—vitality, strength, emotional vigor—all of life becomes available for enjoyment. Not just parts, like one's job, but every moment.

If personal destiny is to be seen in terms of health, we can say that each of us, to a large degree, carves our destiny with knife and fork. Food, after all, is our future—quite literally. Health in its every dimension can be nourished or negated by the mouthful.

Investing in a successful future, then, means learning to eat in ways that produce health.

And what exactly are those ways?

There have been innumerable attempts to define the optimal diet. Raw foods, vegetarian fare, macrobiotics, the four food groups, the American Heart Association diet, the Pritikin diet, all these—and many more—have been put forward as the ideal.

Our approach in *Healthy Cooking* is relatively simple. Here we present recipes for dishes that are generally low in fat, cholesterol, salt and sugars, and high in vitamins, minerals, complex carbohydrates and fiber. That pattern of eating has much to recommend it. Most nutritionally aware physicians believe it helps keep your circulation healthy and your energy level high, and generally tends to prevent a host of symptoms, from digestive problems to bone weakness.

Through recipe testing, we try to ensure that these are not only healthful food ideas, but tasty as well. It's a question not just of pleasure, but also of practicality. After all, just knowing which foods are good investments toward a healthy future is not enough. You've got to eat them! Regularly, just as you work or save money.

Healthy Cooking can be a valuable resource in this endeavor. Become familiar with the book: Browse through it and find some ideas that look interesting. Pay particular attention to foods that your family already likes. And consider which fruits and vegetables are currently in season where you live. Begin with recipes that are relatively simple and don't require that you buy many ingredients or spices you normally don't have on hand.

So: *bon appétit*. And may the joy of eating become the joy of good health!

Executive Editor, **Prevention**® Magazine

1

Eating Right, Eating Well

"What the fool does in the end, the wise man does in the beginning."

Ancient Proverb

"A man too busy to take care of his health is like a mechanic too busy to take care of his tools," said the Roman orator Cicero more than 2,000 years ago. And the same thing still can be said today.

Even though our lifestyles are busier and more harried than ever—packed with careers, family, friends, entertainment, educational programs and hobbies—health is still our bottom line.

Without the stamina, the energy or the vitality to cope, our lives, like the improvident mechanic's occupation, would soon fall to ruin.

And one of the most important ways we have of nurturing our health is through the food we eat. By choosing foods such as fresh fruits and vegetables, whole grains, poultry, fish and lean meats, we give our bodies the proper nutrition to maintain good health.

In fact, even if we have abused our bodies with a poor diet, we still can restore or actually improve our health by making more careful eating choices from now on.

Understand that changing the diet doesn't mean giving up everything we love. Often, a favorite dish needs only a change in cooking method to bring it up to our new health standards. Fresh foods, prepared well and attractively served, easily can replace old standbys and often become new favorites. These not only help to build our bodies but also nurture our spirits.

Rather than being depleted shadows of what nature has to offer, these wholesome ingredients

1

Basic Plain Yogurt

Makes 1 quart

4 cups milk
½ cup yogurt

Scald the milk in a stainless steel, enamel or flameproof glass saucepan by heating it until small bubbles appear around the edges. Do not let the milk boil; remove from heat immediately. Allow to cool slightly.

When the milk has cooled to about 100°F, stir in the yogurt. (If you don't have a thermometer, test the temperature of the milk with your finger. It should feel quite warm but not hot.)

Cover the saucepan. Wrap it well in several layers of terry towels, or place it in an oven with a pilot light. Allow the pan to remain undisturbed for 8 hours, or until the yogurt has set. Store finished yogurt in the refrigerator.

come to us with their full complement of life-enhancing vitamins, minerals and fiber—everything our bodies need to thrive.

And rather than relying on sugar, salt and fat to cover up the dull taste of food that has been over-processed and overcooked, we can begin to taste the full-bodied flavors of real foods. Soon, our new diet is not just a quest for better health but also an adventure in discovering a richly varied cuisine.

FROM MORNING TILL NIGHT

Whether you're just easing into a healthier diet at home, or you've been cooking wholesome meals for some time, you'll find special recipes here that will tickle your taste buds without compromising your health. Even beginning cooks will find the recipes easy to follow and the dishes fairly easy to prepare.

For those living in the fast lane, we realize these meals must fit into full, many-faceted lives. We understand, for example, that weekday breakfasts are often hurried. And so, for breakfasts as well as for other meals, we have provided some quick recipes along with others that can be prepared ahead and served in a wink—and still offer serious nutrition.

And for the few extra minutes you'll be spending doing things from "scratch," remember that this time and effort pays off in both health and great taste. Have no fear of serving any of these meals to guests!

We have, in fact, included several outstanding, rather "gourmet" recipes in this book. These are to be used when entertaining friends, family or even just yourself on some special day. And even though we wouldn't want to have our festive dishes *every* day (their very specialness would soon wear off), it's wonderful to enjoy a treat when the occasion demands it.

We have included, for example, a few recipes using phyllo pastry, traditionally found in Middle Eastern cuisine. While this dough can be homemade or purchased from a Middle Eastern bakery, most people find it most convenient to buy commercially prepared phyllo. It is avail-

able in the refrigerated section of most large supermarkets—next to the tubes of crescent rolls and boxes of puff pastry. The procedures recommended for using phyllo dough are based on the size of commercially available sheets. This very thin dough is usually used in layers. Although it is not whole grain, we feel it can be used in certain festive dishes when a special touch is needed. And if it helps us to cut back on the fatty meats often associated with holidays, we feel it's earned its keep.

For bakers new to trying whole grains, we've incorporated some unbleached flour to give loaves more loft and add a more familiar texture to cakes. The recipes that are all whole grain were chosen for their ease in baking, even for beginners.

RECIPES MARKED FOR SPECIFIC HEALTH BENEFITS

There's another special aspect to this book. You'll notice small symbols alongside many recipes. These point out those dishes analyzed to be exceptional—either very low in fat, low in sodium, high in fiber or high in calcium. Recipes especially suited for entertaining also are marked.

By using these symbols, you can choose specific recipes best suited to your individual needs—those adjusted for particular health problems or those that can help you to prevent certain health problems. In other words, you can develop meals tailor-made to your own health situation. For example:

● **Low-Fat Meals.** Eating less fat aids in the battle against overweight and may protect against heart disease and cancer.

● **Low-Sodium Meals.** Cutting down on salt is believed to be a protective measure against blood pressure problems.

● **High-Fiber Meals.** Fiber may help protect against heart disease, digestive disorders and high blood pressure.

● **High-Calcium Meals.** Maintaining sufficient calcium levels helps protect against osteoporosis and helps ensure proper nerve and muscle function.

● **Meals for Entertaining**. These recipes produce elegant "company" dishes. While they contain neither salt nor wine, these special recipes are not recommended for everyday use.

With their emphasis on whole grains, fresh fruits and vegetables, fish, poultry, elimination of salt and sparing use of red meats, these recipes may be slightly different from the meals to which many of us are accustomed. But it's important to point out that, in terms of health, we don't want to buy "all-American" when it comes to diet. Why not? Because, unfortunately, the typical American diet is higher in fat and sugar than that of nearly any other country in the world. Many scientists have linked this kind of diet with the chronic and often fatal health problems that plague our society: heart disease, obesity, diabetes and cancer of the breast and colon.

Other affluent countries, which share a similar high-fat, high-sugar, low-fiber diet, share similar profiles of these health problems. In so-called underdeveloped nations, meat and refined products such as white flour are either scarce or prohibitively expensive, and there is less dependency on dairy foods and sugar and greater dependency on grains and fresh vegetables. These countries show a minor incidence of these health problems among their population.

FAT CITY— A POOR-HEALTH GHETTO

The American diet is comprised of almost 40 percent fat, the most concentrated source of calories. One gram of fat supplies the body with 9 calories, as compared to only 4 calories per gram of protein or carbohydrates. Our standard fare loads us with about twice the amount of daily dietary fat we actually need for good health. And with fat, as with everything, there are problems with excess.

As a nation we are becoming more conscious of the health problems related to fat. For example, because many of us want to reduce the buildup of cholesterol that has

Making and Using Sprouts

To begin sprouts, place the seeds or beans in a wide-mouth jar. (Be sure these seeds or beans are intended for food; do not use garden seeds, which may have been treated with chemicals.) Cover them generously with water and soak them for several hours. (Larger beans need overnight soaking.) Cover the jar's mouth with a double layer of cheesecloth. Rinse the contents 3 or 4 times a day and drain thoroughly. In 3 to 4 days—*voila!*—sprouts.

Mung Bean Sprouts
Use in stir-frying, Oriental dishes, soups, sandwiches or salads, or mixed with vegetables or rice.

Alfalfa Sprouts
Use in sandwiches or salads, or as a garnish.

Soy Sprouts
Cooked, these can be used in casseroles or main dishes, substituted for chick-peas in hummus, or dried and ground to be used in place of nuts.

Lentil Sprouts
Use in soups, casseroles, main dish salads or breads, or steam them and mix with rice.

been linked with atherosclerosis and heart disease, we have turned to using polyunsaturated fats, such as vegetable oils. However, saturated fat still constitutes a large percentage of the American diet—fat such as that found in dairy products, eggs and meats.

Moreover, substituting polyunsaturated for saturated fat may not be the whole solution to our dietary dilemma. It appears that high levels of *any* fat, even polyunsaturated fat, are undesirable. So what we have to do, then, is cut back on all fat until we more nearly approach the bare minimum (1 tablespoon) required each day to meet basic nutritional needs.

Timetable for Cooking Beans

Wash the beans, cover them generously with water and soak overnight (lentils and split peas need no soaking). Drain, then place the beans in a saucepan and cover with water. Bring the water to a boil, reduce heat and simmer until tender.

TYPE OF BEAN		COOKING TIME
Lentils		45 minutes
Split peas		1 hour
Navy beans		1½ hours
Lima beans		1½ hours
Kidney beans		1½ hours
Black beans		1½ hours
Chick-peas		3 hours
Soybeans		3 hours or more

A WORD ABOUT SALT

None of the recipes in *Healthy Cooking* calls for salt. If your palate is accustomed to the taste of salty food, some of these dishes may seem slightly bland at first. However, if you give them a fair trial, your taste buds will soon adjust—and you'll find delightful nuances of flavor previously overshadowed by salt. This period of adjustment is worth the effort it requires. The payback is in better health. Salt is linked to high blood pressure, which, in turn, can lead to other health problems such as stroke and heart attack.

In addition to using our low-sodium recipes, you might consider these additional suggestions for cutting down on salt:

- Don't salt your food at the table.
- Season your food with spices, herbs or lemon juice.
- Avoid foods with added sodium, such as canned soups, processed foods and luncheon meats.
- Snack on fresh fruits and vegetable sticks.
- Avoid highly salted snack foods such as potato chips and pretzels.

FOOD WITH FIBER

One thing these recipes share is an emphasis on fiber. Dietary fiber is that portion of certain foods that is indigestible and that travels intact through the stomach and intestines. You may wonder what good it can do for you if it's not digested. Well, it does plenty. First of all, because this fiber is not digested, it adds no calories to your daily tally. Although you wouldn't want to eat an entire meal of fiber, eating a moderate amount helps to fill you up—making it easier for you to cut back on other, calorie-rich foods. (You may have noticed, for example, that eating a baked potato with the main course reduces your craving for dessert.)

Perhaps the reason we need fiber is simply this: The human digestive system evolved long before people learned how to mill wheat into white flour or to skin the brown covering from a grain of rice. Today we're faced with "instant" food products that have been so processed that they no longer contain this dietary element. But here we are, with that same old digestive tract—the one that needs fiber to work properly. It helps to speed the movement of wastes through the bowels. This efficient transit time means any toxic or irritating materials spend less time in contact with intestinal linings. In addition, adding bulk to the diet makes the work of the intestines easier. Fiber absorbs water and provides bulk to the food residue that must be eliminated from the body. This loose mixture is easy to eliminate, in contrast to small, compacted residue that makes the bowels work harder to expel it. Researchers attribute diverticulosis, a painful condition of the large intestine, to diets far too low in fiber.

HIGH-CALCIUM RECIPES IDENTIFIED

Recipes developed to provide exceptionally high levels of calcium also have been marked. Calcium is a nutrient of enormous importance—for babies, children, nursing mothers, pregnant women and, perhaps surprisingly, for women past the age of menopause. Of course, we all know that children need calcium for their growing teeth and bones. But why do older women need this mineral? Because sufficient dietary calcium can prevent osteoporosis, a widespread disorder among older women.

With osteoporosis, the bones become brittle and porous, often resulting in back pain and fractures. High calcium intake works wonders to prevent this disorder and may even help restore the bones to their former strength. In addition, calcium keeps the muscles—including the heart muscle—working long and strong.

Foods high in calcium include milk and milk products, soybeans, almonds, broccoli and dark green, leafy vegetables. Many recipes in *Healthy Cooking* are high in calcium. Serve them to young and old alike.

FOOD THAT EARNS APPLAUSE

Of course, you are serving these meals to family and friends for the obvious health benefits that accrue from a healthy diet. But you need not worry about hearing the moans that too often greet a dish that's "good for you." Instead, be prepared for the sound of applause. Moreover, get ready to share with your family and friends the pleasure and excitement of exploring a whole world of delicious healthy foods. Get ready to savor such international dishes as Scones, Paella, German Fresh Fruit Torte, Pierogi, Dutch Pea Soup, or Ratatouille. Try Spanakopita, Chicken Pilau with Currants, or Mexican Meatballs. Or enjoy any of a number of American-style favorites, developed to maximize *your* well-being.

So join us in the kitchen and let us show you how, with these carefully chosen recipes, we can get you on the road and keep you on the road to better health.

Bon appétit!

2

Breakfast: First and Fantastic

The first meal of the day should get you off to a vigorous start.

I deally, 25 percent of the day's calories should be consumed at breakfast. Yet many of us skip what is often called the most important meal of the day.

To really use breakfast to the best advantage, choose foods that will burn slowly all morning, giving you an even source of energy as you work or play.

Your best breakfast bets are foods high in protein and natural, unrefined carbohydrates. These keep your energy level on an even keel. On the other hand, foods high in sugar, accompanied by caffeinated coffee or tea, create a rush of insulin into the bloodstream, which soon pulls blood sugar levels down to below normal. So much for your energy!

Many people rely on bacon, sausage, ham or hash to push up the protein content of breakfast. But whole grains, supplemented by nuts, seeds or dairy products, can do the job, too. These foods, when eaten together, complement each other. They give you the value of meat protein without the calories and fat that accompany the traditional breakfast meats.

Vary your morning diet with flavored yogurts, a ricotta cheese-based sundae, pancakes, crepes, waffles, porridge and granola. Fresh fruit should be included in the morning menu, and possibly an herb tea, as well.

In addition to providing a well-balanced meal, these recipes focus on fiber, the ingredient that helps to keep your digestive tract healthy and lets you know when it's time to stop eating *before* you run the risk of adding pounds. Fiber is nature's natural brake on eating too much.

You'll find enough breakfast ideas here to enjoy for three full weeks of healthful morning meals without a repeat.

7

Breakfast Melon Bowl ●

A refreshing summer breakfast.

Makes 2 servings

 1 medium cantaloupe
¾ cup ricotta cheese
¾ cup yogurt
 2 teaspoons maple syrup
 2 drops lemon extract
½ banana, diced
½ cup blueberries
　　whole strawberries (garnish)
　　mint sprigs (garnish)

Halve the cantaloupe and remove the seeds. In a small bowl, combine the ricotta, yogurt, maple syrup and lemon extract. Stir until smooth.

　　Fold the banana and blueberries into the ricotta mixture. Fill the cantaloupe halves with the cheese and fruit mixture. Garnish with strawberries and mint sprigs, and serve with whole grain muffins or raisin bread.

Hawaiian Ricotta Sundae ● ● ●

A colorful brunch or breakfast dish.

Makes 2 servings

 1 cup ricotta cheese
 1 apple, peeled and shredded
¼ cup yogurt
 2 teaspoons honey
¼ teaspoon ground cinnamon
 2 drops vanilla extract
 2 fresh pineapple rings
 1 cup sliced strawberries
 1 tablespoon finely chopped walnuts

In a small bowl, combine the ricotta with the apple, 2 tablespoons of the yogurt, the honey, cinnamon and vanilla.

　　Place the pineapple rings on two serving plates. Using a spoon, form the ricotta mixture into mounds. Center each mound over a pineapple slice.

　　Cover each serving with strawberries. Top each with a tablespoon of yogurt and dust with nuts. If desired, chill before serving.

You'll think you're in Paradise, breakfasting on a Hawaiian Ricotta Sundae, served here in a pineapple shell. The combination of low-fat cheese and yogurt with fresh fruit makes this a good breakfast choice for dieters.

Peach-Filled German Omelet ●

Makes 2 servings

 1 large ripe peach, halved and pitted
 1 tablespoon apple juice
 1 tablespoon maple syrup
 3 eggs
⅓ cup skim milk
 2 tablespoons whole wheat flour
　　dash of freshly grated nutmeg
 2 teaspoons Butter-Half (page 133)
　　peach slices (garnish)
　　mint sprigs (garnish)

Place half of the peach in a blender with the apple juice and maple syrup. Process on low speed until smooth. Transfer to a small saucepan.

　　Thinly slice the remaining peach half. Gently stir it into the mixture in the saucepan. Heat through, then cover the pan and keep the mixture warm.

Place the eggs, milk, flour and nutmeg in the blender. Process on medium speed until smooth.

Melt 1 teaspoon butter-half in an omelet pan. When it has stopped foaming, add half of the egg mixture. Swirl the pan, pulling the edges of the omelet toward the center of the pan with a table knife. Keep swirling so that the uncooked portion runs to the outside edges of the pan.

When the top of the omelet is no longer runny and the bottom is golden brown, spoon half of the peach mixture down the center. Fold the omelet over the filling, then slip the omelet onto a plate.

Briefly reblend remaining egg mixture and make a second omelet with the remaining ingredients. Garnish with peach slices and mint sprigs.

Fruit-Studded Coffee Cake ●

Dried fruits flavor a hearty cake that's topped with ground almonds. One slice makes a filling breakfast that is especially appealing for those who "don't like breakfast."

⅓ cup chopped dried apricots
⅓ cup chopped pitted prunes
¼ cup dried currants
¾ cup orange juice
¼ cup honey
¼ cup butter, melted
¼ cup sunflower oil
1 egg, beaten
1 teaspoon vanilla extract
1½ cups whole wheat flour
1½ teaspoons baking powder
½ teaspoon ground cinnamon
¼ teaspoon ground coriander
¼ cup ground almonds

In a medium bowl, stir together the apricots, prunes, currants, orange juice, honey, butter, oil, egg and vanilla. Set aside for 20 minutes.

Combine the flour, baking powder, cinnamon and coriander in a large bowl. Stir in the fruit mixture just until combined.

Spread the batter evenly in an oiled 8-inch round cake pan. Sprinkle with almonds.

Bake in a preheated 350°F oven for 35 to 40 minutes, or until cake is golden brown and a knife inserted in the center comes out clean. Cool slightly before serving.

Variation: Omit butter and increase sunflower oil by ¼ cup.

Fruited French Toast
●●

Use fresh fruits of the season to top whole grain french toast. Then sit back and really enjoy your morning.

Makes 4 to 5 servings

3 eggs
½ cup milk
½ teaspoon ground cinnamon
½ teaspoon vanilla extract
8 to 10 slices whole wheat bread
2 cups sliced strawberries, blueberries or sliced peaches
¼ cup maple syrup
    mint sprigs or sliced kiwi fruit
    (garnish)

Place the eggs, milk, cinnamon and vanilla in a blender. Process on medium speed until smooth. Pour the batter into a shallow bowl.

One by one, dip the bread slices in the batter, turning to coat both sides. Cook the dipped bread slices in an oiled skillet until golden brown on both sides. Keep toast warm until all the pieces are done.

For topping, combine the fruit or berries with the maple syrup. Spoon the fruit over the french toast when you serve it, or place the fruit topping in a bowl on the table. Garnish with mint sprigs or kiwi fruit.

Variations: Substitute black or red raspberries. Or try a combination of fruits and eliminate the maple syrup.

Three Ways with French Toast

Make It Thick. Cut home-baked whole wheat bread into slices 1½ inches thick. Soak the slices well in batter, then cook in a buttered skillet until both sides are golden. Pop into a preheated 350°F oven for 15 to 20 minutes, to ensure the center is cooked.

Plan Ahead. Make up a few pieces of french toast, then wrap and freeze them. Warm them up in a toaster before serving.

Try a Banana Batter. Replace some of the liquid in the batter with pureed bananas. For example, when preparing Fruited French Toast, reduce the amount of milk from ½ to ⅓ cup, then blend in half a ripe banana.

9

Orange Whole Wheat Waffles ●

Add a summery dash to a favorite dish—the flavor of orange and the tang of rind.

Makes 4 waffles

1¼ cup whole wheat flour
1½ teaspoons baking powder
  1 teaspoon ground cinnamon
  1 egg, beaten
  3 tablespoons sunflower oil
  1 cup orange juice
½ cup buttermilk or skim milk
  1 teaspoon grated orange rind
⅛ teaspoon almond extract
    orange slices (garnish)

Combine the flour, baking powder and cinnamon in a large bowl.

In a medium bowl, beat together the egg, oil, orange juice, buttermilk or skim milk, orange rind and almond extract. Stir into the dry ingredients just until combined.

Pour the batter onto a hot, lightly oiled waffle iron and bake until cooked throughout. Serve hot, topped with Breakfast Orange Sauce (this page) and garnished with orange slices.

Breakfast Orange Sauce ● ●

A not-too-sweet finishing touch for any of these pancakes or waffles.

Makes 1 cup

  ¾ cup orange juice
  1 tablespoon maple syrup
1½ teaspoons cornstarch
  1 drop almond extract
  1 large navel orange

Heat ½ cup of the orange juice with the maple syrup in a small saucepan over low heat. Next, dissolve the cornstarch in the remaining orange juice. When the maple syrup mixture is nearly boiling, stir in the cold orange juice. Add the almond extract.

Bring the juice to a boil over low heat, then simmer it 2 to 3 minutes, until the sauce thickens. Remove from heat.

Peel the orange, cut it into thin slices and then coarsely chop. Stir into the sauce and heat briefly.

Sour Cream-Carob Waffles ●

Serve these unusual waffles with maple syrup for a special brunch or with fruit and whipped topping for dessert.

Makes 3 waffles

⅓ cup whole wheat flour
⅓ cup unbleached flour
  3 tablespoons carob powder
  1 teaspoon baking powder
⅓ cup sour cream
⅓ cup yogurt
  2 tablespoons sunflower oil
  2 teaspoons light unsulfured
     molasses
  2 eggs, beaten

Combine the flours, carob and baking powder in a medium bowl. In a small bowl, beat together the sour cream, yogurt, oil, molasses and eggs until the mixture is smooth.

Stir the egg mixture into the dry ingredients just until combined.

Pour batter onto a hot, lightly oiled waffle iron and bake until cooked throughout. Serve hot for breakfast, or serve warm or cold for dessert.

Whole grain waffles will get your day off to a wonderful start. Try them with Breakfast Orange Sauce, a sunny, low-calorie topping.

Use Buckwheat Crepes to make cozy pockets for scrambled eggs. These light and airy crepes also can be served like pancakes, with a fruit topping.

Buckwheat Crepes

Makes 12 to 14 crepes

1⅓ cups milk
2 eggs
1 drop vanilla extract
¾ cup buckwheat flour
¼ cup unbleached flour
1 teaspoon ground cinnamon

Place all of the ingredients in a blender and process on low to medium speed until the batter is smooth.

Place the blender container in the refrigerator for 30 minutes. Blend again briefly before cooking.

Pour about 2 tablespoons of the batter into a crepe pan and swirl the pan to cover the bottom with batter.

Cook until the top appears dry. Turn, and cook a few seconds longer. Cool the crepes on a towel-covered wire rack.

Buckwheat Crepes with Eggs and Cheese ●

Usually a delicate dish, these crepes are hale and hearty, packing lots of nutrition and deep-down flavor.

Makes 2 servings

1 teaspoon butter
2 eggs, beaten
3 tablespoons cottage cheese
4 Buckwheat Crepes (opposite page)
2 slices kiwi fruit (garnish)
2 orange slices (garnish)
  watercress sprigs (garnish)

Melt the butter in a medium skillet and add the eggs. Stir occasionally as the eggs cook, and add the cottage cheese just before the eggs are firm.

As soon as the cheese is incorporated into the eggs, remove from heat.

Fold the crepes in half, then in quarters. Lift up the top quarter of the folded crepes and place the egg filling in the pockets. Fold back the top slightly to reveal filling.

Garnish the plates with fruit slices and watercress sprigs.

Almond Milk ●

You can use almond milk as a substitute for whole or skim milk in a wide variety of recipes.

Makes 1 quart

1 cup whole almonds
4 cups water
2 tablespoons maple syrup or honey

Place the almonds and water in a medium saucepan. Bring to a boil, then reduce heat, cover and simmer for 30 minutes.

Place the boiled almonds and half of their cooking liquid in a blender. Process on high speed for 2 minutes.

Strain the mixture into a glass container by pouring it through a sieve. Return any remaining ground almonds in the sieve to the blender and add the maple syrup or honey.

Add the remaining cooking liquid and blend on high speed for 2 minutes. Again strain the liquid.

Press the ground almonds in the sieve with the back of a spoon to release all their liquid into the container. (You can use the leftover ground almonds in baked goods or cooked cereals.)

Store the almond milk in the refrigerator. Shake before using.

NOTE: If you use honey as the sweetener, do not give almond milk to babies under one year of age because of the risk of botulism.

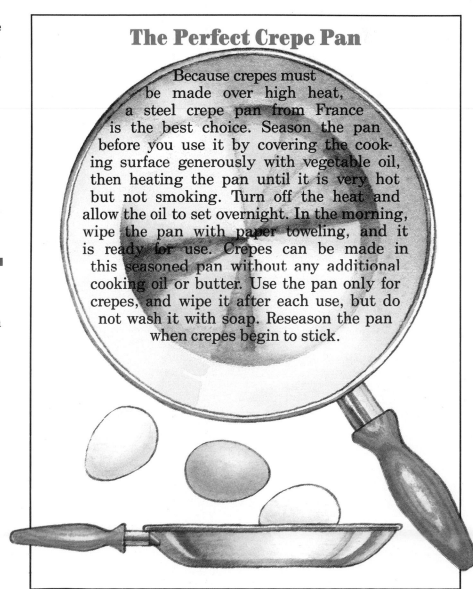

The Perfect Crepe Pan

Because crepes must be made over high heat, a steel crepe pan from France is the best choice. Season the pan before you use it by covering the cooking surface generously with vegetable oil, then heating the pan until it is very hot but not smoking. Turn off the heat and allow the oil to set overnight. In the morning, wipe the pan with paper toweling, and it is ready for use. Crepes can be made in this seasoned pan without any additional cooking oil or butter. Use the pan only for crepes, and wipe it after each use, but do not wash it with soap. Reseason the pan when crepes begin to stick.

Place the milk and water in a medium saucepan. Stir in the cornmeal and wheat germ.

Set the pan over medium heat. Using a wire whisk, stir constantly until the cereal begins to boil.

Reduce heat and partially cover the pan. Simmer for 6 to 8 minutes, stirring frequently.

Stir in the cheese; when it has melted, add the tamari. Remove from heat. Serve with additional milk.

Variation: To make a sweet cornmeal porridge, omit the cheese and tamari. In their place, add maple syrup to taste. Top with your choice of raisins, currants, grated apple or berries, or try sliced peaches, bananas, apricots or crushed pineapple.

Apple-Millet Cereal

● ● ●

Makes 4 to 6 servings

1 cup millet
3 cups water
1 large tart apple
1 to 2 tablespoons maple syrup
  chopped walnuts (garnish)

Place the millet and water in a medium saucepan and bring to a boil over medium heat. Reduce heat, cover and simmer for 45 minutes, stirring occasionally.

While the millet is cooking, core the apple and shred it.

When the millet is soft and the water has been absorbed, stir in the apple. Remove pan from heat. Cover and let stand about 3 minutes.

Serve the cereal with maple syrup and walnuts. If desired, also serve with milk.

NOTE: To reheat, add a little extra water or milk to the cooked cereal in a heavy-bottom saucepan or double boiler. Stir the cereal until it's heated through.

Variation: Prepare an interesting millet pilaf with the leftovers. In a small saucepan, saute some chopped scallions or onions in a mixture of sunflower oil and butter until the

Savory Breakfast Porridge ● ● ●

Almost everyone likes a sweet breakfast cereal, but if you are one who doesn't, try this cornmeal mix flavored with cheddar cheese to get your morning off to a satisfying start.

Makes 2 servings

1 cup milk
1 cup water
⅔ cup stone-ground cornmeal
¼ cup wheat germ
½ cup shredded sharp cheddar cheese
1 teaspoon tamari

onions are soft. Stir in leftover cereal and cook over low heat until it's heated through. If desired, stir in a few toasted sunflower seeds.

Variations: Add raisins, dates, currants or chopped fresh fruit to the cooked oatmeal. Substitute 1 tablespoon ground walnuts for half of the almonds.

Rice Porridge with Apricots ● ● ●

Begin your day with vitamin A-rich apricots cooked into a delicious porridge that needs no sweeteners.

Makes 2 servings

 1 cup cooked brown rice
½ cup apple juice or cider
½ cup water
¼ cup dried apricot halves, chopped

Place the rice, apple juice or cider and water in a medium saucepan. Stir in the apricots.

Bring to a boil, then reduce heat and simmer, covered, 8 to 10 minutes, stirring frequently. Serve when most of the liquid is absorbed.

Variations: Add a small amount of apple juice or cider, or milk, when serving. Add ¼ cup of peeled, grated apple to the rice before cooking, or add it raw when serving. Add other fresh fruits, such as berries, when serving.

Maple-Almond Oatmeal ●

Makes 2 servings

1½ cups water
⅔ cup rolled oats
 2 tablespoons ground almonds
 1 tablespoon maple syrup

Place the water and oats in a small saucepan and bring to a boil. Reduce heat and simmer 1 to 2 minutes.

Stir in the almonds and maple syrup. Cook until the oatmeal reaches the desired consistency. Serve with skim milk or Almond Milk (page 13).

Cream of Rice ● ●

This delicious breakfast porridge can be served with either fresh or dried fruits and further sweetened with a touch of maple syrup.

Makes 4 servings

½ cup uncooked brown rice
 4 cups water
 1 tablespoon maple syrup

Place the rice and water in a medium saucepan and bring to a boil over medium heat. Reduce heat to the lowest setting, cover the pan and cook for 1½ hours, or until the rice is very soft and the mixture looks like thick oatmeal when stirred.

Place the rice mixture, half at a time, in a blender and process on low speed until smooth. Stir in the maple syrup. Serve hot.

NOTE: You can easily double this recipe. Store unblended cooked rice in the refrigerator. Reheat just enough for individual breakfast portions, then blend before serving.

Variations: For *Almond Cream of Rice,* grind ¼ cup of almonds in the blender in short bursts at high speed before adding the cooked rice. For *Strawberry Cream of Rice,* blend in strawberries. You can also vary the recipe by blending in currants, raisins, blueberries or sliced peaches.

When you think of hot cereal, don't limit yourself to oats. Rice, millet and cornmeal also lend themselves to satisfying breakfast fare. Opposite page, from bottom: Rice Porridge with Apricots, Maple-Almond Oatmeal, and Savory Breakfast Porridge. This page, from top: Apple-Millet Cereal and Strawberry Cream of Rice.

Quick-Mix Granola with Nuts ● ●

Avoid the baked-in oils and sweeteners found in commercial granolas by preparing this fresh version. Just mix, then store for future fast breakfasts.

Makes 10 servings

 2 cups rolled oats
 1 cup chopped walnuts or pecans
 1 cup raisins
½ cup wheat germ
¼ cup soy flakes
¼ cup bran
¼ cup sunflower seeds
 2 tablespoons sesame seeds

In a large bowl, stir all of the ingredients together until combined.
    Store in the refrigerator in a jar or tightly covered container.

Variations: Substitute currants for the raisins, pumpkin seeds for the sunflower seeds. Add chopped figs.

Fruited Granola ● ● ●

Makes 4 servings

 1 apple, chopped
 1 pear, chopped
 2 bananas
 1 cup seedless grapes
1⅓ cup Quick-Mix Granola with
        Nuts (this page)
 2 cups yogurt (optional)

Place one-fourth of the chopped apple and pear in each of four serving bowls. Add one-half banana, diced, and ¼ cup of grapes to each bowl.
    Sprinkle the granola over the fruit. The fruit and cereal can be tossed together and eaten as is, or top each serving with ½ cup of yogurt. Granola and fruit can also be served with milk.

Variation: In summer, replace the apple, pear, bananas and grapes with your choice of peaches, berries or nectarines.

Add any fruits you like to Quick-Mix Granola with Nuts to create Fruited Granola—a delicious, high-fiber way to greet the morning.

Lemon Yogurt ● ● ●

Makes 1 serving

1 cup yogurt
2 teaspoons maple syrup
⅛ teaspoon lemon extract
    thin lemon slice (garnish)
    mint sprig (garnish)

Combine the yogurt, maple syrup and lemon extract in a small bowl until well mixed.

Serve chilled, garnished with lemon and mint.

NOTE: See page 2 for directions for making Basic Plain Yogurt.

Strawberry Yogurt

Makes 2 servings

1 cup frozen whole strawberries
1 cup yogurt
1 tablespoon maple syrup
1 drop vanilla extract

Allow the strawberries to thaw. Place the yogurt in a small bowl, then stir the strawberries, maple syrup and vanilla into the yogurt.

Continue stirring until the strawberries are mashed and the yogurt is bright pink in color.

NOTE. Frozen strawberries, rather than fresh, are used to achieve a softer consistency that allows them to be easily incorporated into the yogurt.

Flavor your own yogurts to your own liking. Carob, strawberry and lemon are all delicious. Add chunks of fresh fruit for a quick luncheon.

Carob Yogurt ● ●

Makes 1 serving

1 cup yogurt
2 teaspoons maple syrup
2 teaspoons carob powder
¼ teaspoon vanilla extract

Place the yogurt in a small bowl. Add the maple syrup, carob and vanilla and stir until well combined.

Variation: For *Vanilla Yogurt,* eliminate the carob powder and double the vanilla extract.

Cinnamon–Apple Pancakes ● ● ●

Here's a double-apple pancake. Blended apples flavor the batter; sliced apples are baked right in.

Makes 16 pancakes

1 cup diced tart red apples
2 eggs
1 cup skim milk
1 cup apple juice or cider
1 tablespoon sunflower oil
2 cups whole wheat flour
2 teaspoons baking powder
1 teaspoon ground cinnamon
1 tart red apple, thinly sliced

Place the diced apples, eggs, milk, apple juice or cider and oil in a blender. Process on medium speed until smooth.

Combine the flour, baking powder and cinnamon in a medium bowl. Stir in the apple mixture just until combined. Do not overmix.

For each pancake, pour about ¼ cup of batter onto a lightly oiled griddle. Top each pancake with a few slices of apple before the top has a chance to set.

When the bubbles that form on the top of the pancake have burst and the bottom is well browned, turn the pancake and cook until the second side is browned. If desired, serve with Honey-Apple Topping (page 21).

Blueberry-Cornmeal Pancakes ● ●

Makes 16 pancakes

1½ cups stone-ground cornmeal
½ cup whole wheat flour
½ cup brown rice flour
2 teaspoons baking powder

Plain pancakes? Not for you! Try Whole Wheat Pancakes, enriched with brown rice flour and wheat germ, Blueberry-Cornmeal or Cinnamon-Apple for variety and great taste.

½ teaspoon baking soda
2 eggs, beaten
3 tablespoons corn oil
1½ to 2 cups buttermilk
¾ cup blueberries

Place the cornmeal, flours, baking powder and soda in a large bowl. In a small bowl, combine the eggs and corn oil.

Stir egg mixture and 1½ cups buttermilk into the dry ingredients just until combined. Add additional buttermilk if batter is too thick.

For each pancake, pour about ¼ cup of batter onto a lightly oiled griddle. Sprinkle each pancake with some of the blueberries.

When the bubbles that form on the top of the pancake have burst and the bottom is well browned, turn the pancake and cook until the second side is browned.

Whole Wheat Pancakes ●

Makes 20 pancakes

2 cups whole wheat flour
½ cup brown rice flour
¼ cup wheat germ
2 teaspoons baking powder
2 eggs, beaten
2¼ cups whole milk
2 tablespoons sunflower oil

Combine the flours, wheat germ and baking powder in a large bowl.

In a small bowl, combine the eggs, milk and oil. Stir gently into the dry ingredients, just until combined.

Pour about ¼ cup of batter for each pancake onto a lightly oiled griddle. When the bubbles that form on the top of the pancake have burst and the bottom is well browned, turn the pancake and cook until the second side is browned. Serve hot, with Strawberry Sauce (page 20).

Toppings and Sauces

Substituting a sauce made from fresh fruit for the usual syrup adds vitamins, minerals and fiber to the meal. Serve these sauces over waffles, pancakes and crepes.

Apple-Prune Butter

●●

Tastes like traditional apple butter, but without the added sugar! Make this in autumn or winter, when apples and apple cider are plentiful.

Makes 1½ cups

¼ cup pitted prunes
1½ cups apple cider
2 cups chopped apples
½ teaspoon ground cinnamon
⅛ teaspoon ground allspice
dash of ground cloves

Place the prunes and cider in a small saucepan. Bring to a boil, then reduce heat and simmer, uncovered, for about 30 minutes, or until the prunes are completely soft. Be careful to *simmer,* or the cider may boil away. There should be some liquid left with the cooked prunes.

Place the prunes and liquid in a blender with the apples and spices. Process on medium speed until smooth, stopping to scrape down the sides as necessary.

Place the blended mixture in a small saucepan. Bring to a simmer and cook over low heat, stirring frequently, until quite thick, 20 to 30 minutes.

Pack in a sterilized jar and store, tightly covered, in the refrigerator.

Strawberry Sauce

●●

Serve over whole grain pancakes, waffles and desserts.

Makes 2 cups

2 cups strawberries
⅓ cup maple syrup

Place the strawberries and maple syrup in a blender, or a food processor fitted with the steel blade.

Process until smooth on low, then medium speed in the blender, or about 30 seconds in the food processor.

To serve warm over pancakes, waffles or French toast, place the sauce in a small saucepan over low heat. Stir frequently until heated through.

To serve as a dessert sauce, chill thoroughly.

Honey Butter ●

Serve this special honey-flavored butter at party brunches and holiday breakfasts.

Makes ½ cup

¼ cup butter, softened
¼ cup honey
   orange slice (garnish)

Using a wooden spoon, cream the butter and honey together in a medium bowl until thoroughly combined. Pack the mixture into a small crock or baking ramekin. Chill until serving time.

   To garnish, cut the orange slice from one edge to the center. Twist the ends in opposite directions and stand the slice atop the butter.

NOTE: You can reduce the saturated fat content of this recipe by half if you substitute Butter-Half (page 133) for the butter.

Variations: Make *Orange Honey Butter* by creaming ½ teaspoon grated orange rind into the mixture. Make *Cinnamon Honey Butter* by adding 1 teaspoon ground cinnamon and a drop of vanilla extract to the basic recipe.

Honey-Apple Topping ● ●

This easy topping is loaded with valuable vitamins and fiber. Serve it over waffles, pancakes or desserts for a touch of sweetness.

Makes 1 cup

 2 tart apples, chopped
⅓ cup apple juice or cider
 2 tablespoons honey
   dash of ground cinnamon

Place all of the ingredients in a blender and process on low to medium speed until smooth.

   If desired, warm the topping in a small saucepan over low heat before serving.

Variations: Use other fruit juices in place of the apple juice or cider for a change of flavor. Substitute light molasses or maple syrup for the honey. Add a dash of freshly grated nutmeg or ground allspice.

3

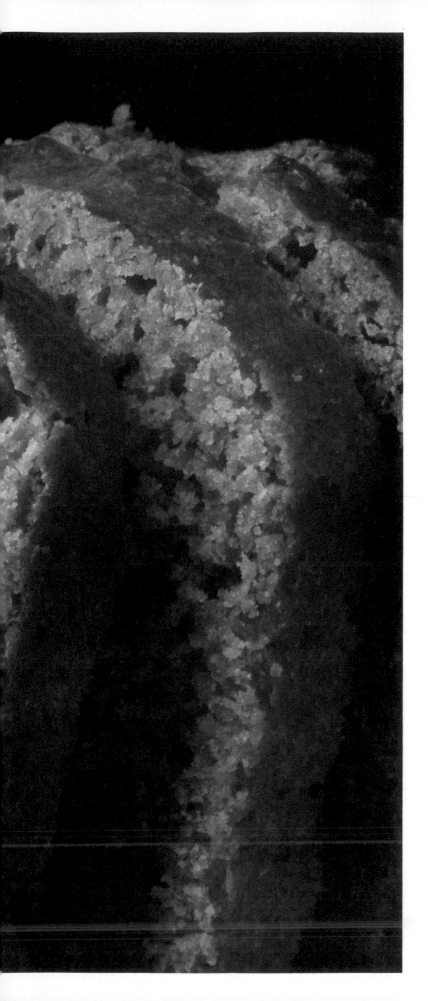

Breads, Rolls and Muffins

For novice or expert, these wholesome loaves are easy to prepare and a loving treat for family and friends.

If there is one aroma that's most likely to prompt a sense of well-being, it's the heavenly smell of bread in the oven. Those of us lucky enough to have had grandmothers who baked know the experience of entering a warm kitchen and being embraced by that special aroma.

But the real treat found in freshly baked bread isn't the smell, it's the taste. And there is something else, too. If you buy bread, it is nearly impossible to escape the dough conditioners, preservatives, hydrogenated oils and other additives you'd rather avoid. But bake your bread at home, and the only ingredients that go into it are those of your own choosing.

Baking yeasted breads, especially with whole grains, takes a bit of skill. To make it easier for you, we've added some unbleached flour to the bread dough. This addition makes the dough easier to knead. It also helps to develop the elasticity of the gluten, allowing the bread to rise. You will find complete directions for making yeasted breads in this chapter, along with a variety of unusual recipes.

In addition to yeasted breads, we have included quick breads, muffins and some specialty breads. The variety is suited to all kinds of entertaining. For example, Scones or Lemon-Glazed Tea Bread are great for a tea party.

Pesto Party Bread Ring serves well at a buffet, while Whole Wheat Popovers are great for a special dinner. Spread peanut butter on a slice of Banana-Pecan Bread for a quick and nutritious breakfast.

Enjoy the aromas of freshly baked breads in your kitchen—but best of all, enjoy their taste!

Oatmeal-Raisin Bread ● ●

Makes 2 loaves

  1 cup raisins
½ cup apple juice or cider
  1 tablespoon ground cinnamon
    dash of freshly grated nutmeg
  2 cups milk
  2 cups rolled oats
½ cup honey
  2 tablespoons butter
  1 tablespoon active dry yeast
¼ cup lukewarm water
2½ cups whole wheat flour
  2 to 2½ cups unbleached flour
  2 tablespoons butter, melted

Place the raisins, apple juice or cider and spices in a small saucepan and bring to a boil. Turn off heat, cover the pan and set aside for 15 minutes.

Meanwhile, place the milk in a medium saucepan and heat until just below the boiling point. Combine the hot milk with the oats, honey and butter in a large bowl. Stir, then let the mixture stand until the butter has melted.

Dissolve the yeast in the water. When the oats mixture has cooled to lukewarm, stir the yeast into the oats. Add the soaked raisins and their liquid.

Stir in the whole wheat flour and beat for 1 minute with a wooden spoon. Then knead in enough unbleached flour to make a smooth dough. Place dough in a large, lightly oiled bowl, turn it to oil all sides, cover with a cloth and let rise in a warm, draft-free place until doubled in bulk.

Punch down the dough, divide it in half and knead each half into an oblong piece. Place each piece in an oiled 8½ × 4½-inch loaf pan. Cover the pans and allow dough to rise in a warm place until nearly doubled in bulk.

Brush loaves with melted butter and bake in a preheated 375°F oven for 45 to 50 minutes, or until they are browned and sound hollow when tapped. Remove loaves from pans and cool on wire racks before cutting.

Apple Cider-Bran Bread ● ●

This recipe offers a delicious opportunity to provide more bran in the diet.

Makes 2 round loaves

  2 cups whole wheat pastry flour
½ cup brown rice flour
1¼ cups unbleached flour
⅓ cup bran
¼ cup sunflower seeds
  2 teaspoons ground cinnamon
    dash of ground mace
  1 cup apple cider
  1 tablespoon active dry yeast
  2 tablespoons maple syrup or honey
  3 tablespoons corn oil
  1 egg
  1 egg white, lightly beaten

Combine the whole wheat and rice flours with 1¼ cups of the unbleached flour in a large bowl. Stir in the bran. Place the sunflower seeds in a blender and grind them with short bursts at high speed. Stir the seeds into the flour mixture, along with the cinnamon and mace.

Place the apple cider in a small saucepan and heat to lukewarm. Place the yeast in a medium bowl and pour the cider over it. Add the maple syrup or honey. When the yeast mixture is foamy, stir in the oil and egg.

Add the yeast mixture to the dry ingredients and stir to combine. Knead on a lightly floured surface for 10 minutes, or until the dough is smooth.

Set the dough in a large, lightly oiled bowl, turn it to oil all sides and cover with a cloth. Allow to rise until doubled in bulk.

Punch down the dough and divide it in half. Knead each half briefly to form a round loaf. Place loaves on a baking sheet and brush with egg white. Allow to rise until nearly doubled in bulk.

Bake in a preheated 350°F oven for 50 to 60 minutes, or until the loaves are browned and sound hollow when tapped.

How to Make Bread

Have all ingredients at room temperature. Dissolve the active dry yeast in a liquid that's been heated to lukewarm, about 105 to 115°F. (If you don't have a thermometer, test the liquid with your finger; it should be quite warm, but not burning hot.) When the yeast mixture is foamy, add any other liquids and stir in about half the flour.

Beat this batter for 1 minute with a wooden spoon. Stir in as much of the remaining flour as you can. When the dough begins to leave the sides of the bowl, turn it out onto a lightly floured work surface. Cover the dough with a cloth and let it rest about 15 minutes. Then oil your fingers and knead the dough until it is smooth and elastic.

Knead by folding the farthest edge of the dough toward the center. Press it down and away from you with the heels of both hands. Give the dough a quarter turn and repeat. (Kneading develops the gluten in the wheat flour, which gives dough its "stretchy" quality and allows it to rise as the yeast cells grow.) Form the dough into a ball.

Oil a bowl large enough to hold the dough after it's doubled. Add the dough ball and turn it over to coat the top surface with oil, so the dough won't dry out.

Cover the bowl with a cloth and set it in a warm, draft-free place to rise. (You can use your oven. Turn on the heat for half a minute, until it's

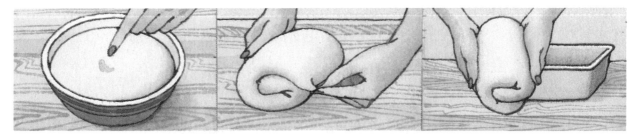

just barely warm. Be sure to remove dough before preheating the oven!) Allow dough to double in bulk. (When the dough is sufficiently risen, the imprint of your fingertips will remain in it when you press them in.) Punch down the dough to remove all the air.

Divide the dough into the portions called for in your recipe. Cover it again while you oil the

pans. Fold the sections of dough into rough rectangles, then place each in an oiled pan, seam-side down. Press the dough down so it touches all sides of the pan. Cover with a cloth, place it in a warm spot and let it rise again until almost doubled in bulk. Bake according to recipe instructions.

Serve the bread slightly warm.

Whole Wheat Bagels
● ●

Makes 1½ dozen

    1 medium potato, quartered
1½ cups skim milk
    2 tablespoons active dry yeast
    1 tablespoon light unsulfured
        molasses
    2 eggs, lightly beaten
    2 cups unbleached flour
    3 to 3½ cups whole wheat flour
        stone-ground cornmeal
    1 egg white, lightly beaten

Place the potato and milk in a small saucepan and bring to a boil. Reduce heat, cover and simmer for 15 minutes, or until the potato is tender.

Place potato mixture in a blender and process on medium speed until smooth. Add a little water, if needed, to make 2 cups.

When the potato mixture has cooled to lukewarm, place it in a large bowl. Add the yeast and molasses. When the yeast mixture is foamy, stir in the eggs and unbleached flour.

Stir in 3 cups of the whole wheat flour, ½ cup at a time, with a wooden spoon. When the dough becomes too stiff to stir, turn it out onto a floured surface and knead in just enough extra flour to make a firm dough.

Knead the dough for 5 to 8 minutes, or until smooth. Then place the dough in a large, lightly oiled bowl and turn it to oil all sides. Cover with a cloth, set in a warm place and allow to rise until doubled in bulk.

Punch down the dough and knead briefly. Divide the dough into 18 equal pieces. On a lightly floured surface, roll each piece into a rope that's about 5 to 6 inches long and tapered at the ends.

Form these ropes into circles by overlapping the ends and moistening them with a few drops of water, if necessary, to make them hold together. Set the formed circles on cookie sheets and allow to rise for approximately 15 minutes.

Fill a large pot with cold water and bring the water to a boil. After the bagels have risen, drop five or six at a time into the boiling water.

After the bagels have floated to the surface, let them boil for a minute or two. Then flip them over and boil for another 2 or 3 minutes. Remove the bagels with a slotted spoon and allow them to drain on a wire cake rack.

Sprinkle two baking sheets with cornmeal. Place the bagels on the baking sheets, brush them with egg white and bake in a preheated 400°F oven for about 40 minutes, or until golden brown.

Whole Wheat Popovers ● ●

These hollow little breads add elegance to any meal.

Makes 1 dozen

3 eggs
1 cup skim milk
3 tablespoons butter, melted
1 cup whole wheat pastry flour

Place the eggs in a medium bowl and beat with a wire whisk or an electric mixer on medium speed until foamy.

Add the milk, butter and flour; continue to beat until the batter is smooth. Divide it evenly among 12 lightly oiled cups of a muffin tin.

Bake the popovers in a preheated 375°F oven for 40 to 45 minutes, until they've "popped" and are golden brown. Don't open the oven door to peek at the popovers until they have baked at least 35 minutes, because the cooler air may prevent them from rising.

Plain Whole Wheat Rolls ●

Use these rolls for Vegetarian Burgers (page 122) or for any other burgers, for that matter. They'll add valuable fiber while providing a hearty flavor.

Makes 1½ dozen

  2 tablespoons active dry yeast
  ½ cup lukewarm water
  3 tablespoons honey
  2 tablespoons tamari
  1 cup buttermilk
1½ cups water
  ½ cup sunflower oil
3½ cups unbleached flour
3½ to 4 cups whole wheat flour

In a large bowl, dissolve the yeast in the lukewarm water. Then stir in the honey and tamari and set the bowl aside.

Heat the buttermilk, 1½ cups of water and oil in a small saucepan until lukewarm. When the yeast mixture is foamy, stir in the buttermilk mixture, the unbleached flour and enough of the whole wheat flour to make a dough that will hold together.

Knead dough on a lightly floured surface until smooth, then form it into 18 balls. Knead each ball until smooth, then place the balls about 2 inches apart on two or three baking sheets.

Let the rolls rise until they are nearly doubled in bulk, then bake in a preheated 400°F oven for 10 minutes. Reduce heat to 350°F and bake an additional 15 to 20 minutes, or until the rolls are lightly browned and sound hollow when tapped.

Cool the rolls on wire racks, covered loosely with foil or a cloth.

Apple Bread Surprise ●

A prize-winning specialty bread with the unexpected taste of caraway.

Makes 1 loaf

2 cups whole wheat flour
1 teaspoon baking powder
½ teaspoon baking soda
½ cup butter
¼ cup honey
¼ cup shredded sharp cheddar cheese
1 cup applesauce
2 eggs
½ cup chopped walnuts
1½ teaspoons caraway seeds

Stir together the flour, baking powder and baking soda in a large bowl.

Heat the butter and honey in a medium saucepan, stirring occasionally, until the butter is melted. Remove from heat.

Stir in cheese until it melts. Incorporate the applesauce, then beat in the eggs, one at a time. Add the walnuts and caraway seeds.

Stir the cheese mixture into the dry ingredients just until combined. Do not overmix.

Transfer the batter to a lightly oiled 8½ × 4½-inch loaf pan. Bake in a preheated 350°F oven for 1 hour, until golden brown.

Variations: You can use raw applesauce if you wish. Just blend chopped apples with a little apple juice until smooth. Also, you can substitute ½ cup sunflower oil for the butter. Heat with the honey, then proceed as directed.

Best Blueberry Muffins ● ● ●

A special muffin with a hint of orange.

Makes 1 dozen

1½ cups whole wheat pastry flour
1 cup wheat germ
2½ teaspoons baking powder
1 cup blueberries
2 eggs
⅓ cup maple syrup
1 orange
½ to ⅔ cup buttermilk
2 tablespoons safflower oil

Stir together the flour, wheat germ and baking powder in a large bowl. Add the blueberries.

In a medium bowl, beat the eggs lightly, then stir in the maple syrup.

Finely grate the rind from the orange and set aside. Squeeze the juice from the orange and add enough buttermilk to make ¾ cup.

Stir the orange rind, buttermilk mixture and oil into the egg mixture. Add this to the dry ingredients. Stir just until combined. Do not overmix.

Divide the batter evenly among 12 lightly oiled cups of a muffin tin. Bake in a preheated 400°F oven for 20 to 25 minutes, until golden brown.

Orange Spice Bread
●●

A quick bread that's a fine accompaniment to herb teas!

Makes 1 loaf

½ cup butter, melted
½ cup honey
½ cup orange juice
½ cup skim milk
2 eggs
1½ teaspoons grated orange rind
¼ teaspoon almond extract
2 cups whole wheat pastry flour
⅓ cup unbleached flour
2 teaspoons baking powder
¼ teaspoon ground allspice
¼ teaspoon ground cardamom
⅛ teaspoon freshly grated nutmeg

In a large bowl, combine the butter, honey and orange juice. Stir in the milk, then beat in the eggs until well combined. Add the almond extract and orange rind.

In a medium bowl, combine the flours, baking powder and spices. Stir the dry ingredients into the orange juice mixture just until combined.

Pour the batter into a lightly oiled 8½ × 4½-inch loaf pan. Bake in a preheated 350°F oven for 55 to 60 minutes, until a cake tester or knife inserted in the center comes out clean. Cool on a cake rack.

Variation: Add 1 cup coarsely chopped pecans to the dry ingredients before adding them to the orange juice mixture.

Currant–Buttermilk Biscuit

An unusual bread, this one large biscuit mixes in minutes and should be eaten piping hot from the oven.

Makes 2 to 3 servings

½ cup whole wheat flour
½ cup unbleached flour
½ teaspoon baking soda
½ teaspoon baking powder
¼ teaspoon ground cinnamon
¼ cup cold butter
2 tablespoons currants
¼ cup buttermilk
1 tablespoon honey

Combine the flours, baking soda, baking powder and cinnamon in a medium bowl or a food processor. Cut the butter into pieces, then mix with the flour, using two knives, a pastry blender or several on-and-off turns of the processor.

When the dry ingredients resemble coarse meal, stir in the currants, buttermilk and honey. Form the dough into a large ball. Place it in a lightly oiled 8-inch cake pan.

Bake the biscuit for 15 minutes in a preheated 350°F oven. Then, using a sharp paring knife, cut an "X" in the top of the biscuit about 1 inch deep. Bake an additional 25 to 30 minutes, or until golden brown.

Variation: Add ¼ teaspoon grated orange rind to the dry ingredients. Substitute 2 tablespoons finely chopped raisins for the currants.

marjoram.

Garlic.

Basil.

Herbed Croutons

Homemade whole wheat bread, with its delicious, dense texture, makes superb croutons. For 3 cups of croutons, cut 4 thick slices of bread into ½-inch or smaller cubes. Spread them out on a baking sheet and dry them in a 200°F oven. Stir the cubes occasionally for even drying.

When you think the cubes are sufficiently dry, turn off the oven and leave the bread in the oven until cool. Croutons must be hard and crisp.

Heat ¼ cup olive oil in a large heavy skillet over medium heat. Add 3 halved, peeled garlic cloves. Stir the garlic until it just begins to turn golden. (Do not let it brown or it will taste bitter.) Toss in the bread cubes and stir them quickly in the oil. Continue stirring over low to medium heat until the oil has been absorbed and the croutons are hot. Remove the garlic.

Place 2 tablespoons grated Parmesan cheese, 1 teaspoon dried marjoram and ¼ teaspoon dried basil in a small paper bag. Add the hot croutons and shake well to coat them with seasonings. Cool the croutons on wire racks covered with paper towels. Store in a large covered jar in a cool, dry place.

Onion-Dill Bread ● ●

Makes 2 round loaves

        1 cup finely chopped onions
        3 tablespoons olive oil
        ⅓ cup minced fresh dill
        1 cup buttermilk
        1 tablespoon honey
        1 tablespoon active dry yeast
        1 egg
        ½ cup wheat germ
        1 cup unbleached flour
        2¼ to 2½ cups whole wheat flour
        1 egg yolk
        1 tablespoon cream or milk
          dill seeds
          celery seeds

In a medium skillet, saute the onions in the oil until translucent and slightly tender. Add the dill and stir over low heat until it is wilted. Set aside.

Heat the buttermilk in a small saucepan until it just reaches the boiling point. (It will appear curdled.) Remove from heat and stir in the honey. Let cool to lukewarm, then stir in the yeast. When the yeast mixture is foamy, mix in the egg.

Mix the wheat germ and unbleached flour in a large bowl. Add 1 cup of whole wheat flour.

Add the buttermilk mixture and onions to the dry ingredients. Beat by hand or with an electric mixer until the dough is "stretchy."

Stir in enough of the remaining whole wheat flour to make a kneadable dough. Knead on a lightly floured surface until smooth.

Place the dough in a large, lightly oiled bowl and turn it to oil all sides. Cover with a cloth and allow to rise in a warm place until almost doubled in bulk.

Punch down the dough and divide it in half. Knead each piece into a round loaf. Place the loaves on a lightly oiled baking sheet. Cover and allow to rise until almost doubled in bulk.

Mix the egg yolk and cream or milk in a small bowl, then brush it on the tops of the bread. Sprinkle with dill seeds and celery seeds.

Bake in a preheated 350°F oven for 35 to 40 minutes, or until the loaves are golden brown and sound hollow when tapped.

Sunflower Seed, Raisin and Bran Muffins ●

Makes 1 dozen

    2 cups whole wheat flour
    ¾ cup bran
    2 teaspoons baking powder
    1 teaspoon ground cinnamon
    ½ cup raisins
    ¼ cup sunflower seeds
    1 cup milk
    ⅓ cup honey
    ⅓ cup sunflower oil
    1 egg

Combine the flour, bran, baking powder, cinnamon, raisins and sunflower seeds in a large bowl.

   Mix the milk, honey, oil and egg in a medium bowl. Add to dry ingredients and stir just until combined. Do not overmix.

   Divide the batter evenly among 12 lightly oiled cups of a muffin tin. Bake in a preheated 400°F oven for about 20 minutes, until golden brown.

Pesto Party Bread Ring ● ●

Flavorful pesto is laced throughout a handsome ring of fresh-baked whole wheat bread. A superb accompaniment to Italian foods.

Makes 18 servings

    2 tablespoons active dry yeast
    ½ cup lukewarm water
    1 tablespoon light unsulfured
        molasses
    1 tablespoon tamari
    2½ cups buttermilk
    ½ cup olive oil
    1 cup wheat germ
    2 cups unbleached flour
    5½ to 6 cups whole wheat flour
    1 cup Pesto Sauce (page 108)

Mix the yeast, water, molasses and tamari in a large bowl. Set aside.

   Heat the buttermilk and olive oil in a small saucepan until lukewarm.

Bake a crusty loaf of Onion-Dill Bread. Flavored with fresh onion, dill and buttermilk, the bread is generously sprinkled with dill and celery seeds for added flavor.

   When the yeast mixture is foamy, stir in the buttermilk mixture, wheat germ and unbleached flour. Beat by hand or with an electric mixer for about 5 minutes.

   Stir in enough whole wheat flour to form a kneadable dough. Turn out onto a lightly floured surface and knead until smooth, about 3 minutes.

   Break off pieces of dough about half the size of a golf ball. Coat each with some of the pesto sauce. Layer the balls evenly in a buttered bundt pan or tube pan.

   Cover the pan with a cloth and allow the dough to rise in a warm place until nearly doubled in bulk.

   Bake in a preheated 350°F oven for 45 minutes, or until golden brown.

Teatime

Scones ● ●

While not as lofty as traditional scones, these are equally high in flavor and texture. Moreover, they're easily made by hand or in a food processor.

Makes 1 dozen

 1 cup whole wheat flour
¾ cup unbleached flour
 2 teaspoons baking powder
¼ cup cold butter
 2 eggs
⅓ cup heavy cream

In a large bowl, stir together the flours and baking powder. Using two knives, a pastry blender or several on-and-off turns of a food processor, cut the butter into the dry ingredients until mixture resembles coarse meal.

Beat the eggs in a small bowl. Add the cream and stir well to combine. Set aside 2 tablespoons of the egg mixture to use as a glaze.

Combine the egg mixture with the dry ingredients. If you are working by hand, do this by making a well in the middle of the dry ingredients, then using a few quick strokes to stir in the egg mixture. Work the dough as little as possible. If you are using a food processor, add the egg mixture all at once and process with a few quick on-and-off turns.

Turn the dough out onto a lightly floured surface and pat it down to about ½ inch thick. Cut it into 2¼-inch rounds with a cookie cutter or inverted glass that's been lightly dusted with flour.

Place the scones on a lightly oiled cookie sheet. Brush tops lightly with the reserved egg mixture.

Bake in a preheated 450°F oven for 15 minutes, or until the scones are lightly browned.

Scones are best served warm. Split them open and serve with butter or homemade fruit preserves.

Banana-Pecan Bread ● ●

Makes 2 loaves

2½ cups whole wheat flour
 1 cup unbleached flour
¼ cup brown rice flour
½ cup bran
 4 teaspoons ground cinnamon
2½ teaspoons baking powder
 1 cup butter
 1 cup honey

3 cups mashed very ripe bananas
4 eggs, lightly beaten
½ cup yogurt
1 cup chopped pecans

In a large bowl, combine the flours.
Add the bran, cinnamon and baking
powder.

Melt the butter in a small
saucepan. Remove from heat and stir
in the honey.

Add the butter mixture, bananas,
eggs, yogurt and pecans to the dry
ingredients and stir just until
combined.

Divide the batter between two
lightly oiled 9 × 5-inch loaf pans.
Bake in a preheated 350°F oven for 1
hour, or until a cake tester or knife
inserted in the center comes out
clean.

Lemon-Glazed Tea Bread ●

Makes 1 loaf

6 tablespoons butter
⅓ cup maple syrup
1 cup whole wheat pastry flour
¾ cup unbleached flour

¾ teaspoon baking soda
½ teaspoon baking powder
⅓ cup buttermilk
2 eggs, lightly beaten
1 tablespoon grated lemon rind
   dash of freshly grated nutmeg
1 teaspoon lemon juice
1 tablespoon honey

In a small saucepan, melt the butter
over low heat. Remove from heat and
stir in the maple syrup. Set aside.

In a large bowl, combine the
flours with the baking soda and
baking powder. Add the butter
mixture, buttermilk, eggs, lemon
rind and nutmeg. Stir until combined.

Place the batter in a lightly oiled
8½ × 4½-inch loaf pan. Bake in a
preheated 350°F oven for 35 minutes,
or until the loaf is golden brown and
a cake tester or knife inserted in the
center comes out clean.

Remove the bread from the pan
and place it on a wire rack set over a
plate. Combine the lemon juice and
honey for a glaze, then spoon it slowly
over the surface of the bread. Reuse
any glaze that collects on the plate.

For easy slicing, allow the bread
to cool completely. Wrap and refrigerate any unused bread to retain its
moisture content.

4

Salads for All Seasons

Salads are natural hot-weather coolers. But they have a place the year 'round.

S alad days are summer days. And, indeed, a crisp green salad spiked with fresh herbs is a great meal on a hot day. Other dishes that don't wilt in the heat and humidity include a Greek salad featuring feta cheese, Orange-Tarragon Potato Salad, or zesty Zucchini and Pink Grapefruit Salad.

But remember that salads can be adapted to any meal of the day, any season of the year. In autumn, try Apple-Walnut Coleslaw or Cabbage-Grape-Pecan Salad. Make a colorful arrangement with Avocado and Cherry Tomato Salad and garnish with watercress.

Winter is a time for hearty salads. Beet and Carrot Salad with Ginger uses vegetables in season as a delicious appetizer. Lentil and Walnut Salad, on the other hand, holds its own as a main dish.

Spring brings a new twist—Fiddlehead Fern Salad. Early garden crops provide the makings for Strawberry and Red Onion Salad, or Asparagus Salad with Pine Nuts. Either will help shake off the old vestiges of winter!

Salads provide some of the best ways we know of to enjoy raw food. And eating raw food has several advantages.

For one thing, raw food is often more nutritious than the same food when it has been cooked. Cauliflower, for example, has more potassium, calcium, iron, thiamine, niacin and vitamin C when it is raw. Some of each of these nutrients is lost when the vegetable is cooked.

And raw vegetables also may provide protection against high blood pressure, diabetes, weight gain and even certain cancers. Salads, in fact, provide you with the one sure opportunity to benefit from a raw deal!

35

Clockwise from top right:
Loose-leaf lettuce, basil leaves,
Buttercrunch lettuce leaf, white-
veined and red-veined Swiss
chard, borage blossom and
nasturtium blossoms, Malabar
spinach, beet leaf, nasturtium
leaves and flower bud, Great
Lakes lettuce, flatleaf parsley,
and Oakleaf lettuce, center.

Herb and Endive Salad ● ●

Makes 4 servings

2 large Belgian endives
2 scallions
  small bunch fresh chives
1 tablespoon lemon juice
¼ cup olive oil
1 teaspoon coarse-grained French
      mustard
  dill sprigs (garnish)

Cut each endive in half lengthwise. Beginning at the base of each half, use a sharp knife to cut toward the top. Keep part of the base intact and spread the endive half open, like a fan. Place on individual serving plates.

Cut the green scallion tops on the diagonal into 1-inch lengths. (Save the white bulbs of the scallions for another purpose.) Place the sliced scallions at the base of the endive halves.

Cut the chives to about the same length as the endive halves. Place about six lengths of chive over the endive halves, also in a fan arrangement.

Prepare the dressing by combining the lemon juice, oil and mustard. Spoon some of the dressing over each salad. Garnish each plate with dill sprigs and serve immediately.

Marinated Green Salad ● ● ●

Makes 6 servings

1 sweet red pepper
1 cup shredded endive or chicory
1 cup cherry tomatoes
¼ cup minced fresh parsley
4 radishes, thinly sliced
1 tablespoon minced fresh chives
¼ cup tarragon vinegar
2 tablespoons water
1 tablespoon lemon juice
1 tablespoon honey

Cut the pepper into thin strips 2 inches long. Place in a serving bowl with the endive or chicory, cherry tomatoes, parsley, radishes and chives.

In a small bowl, mix together the vinegar, water, lemon juice and honey. Pour over the salad ingredients and toss to coat. Cover the bowl tightly and chill for 1 hour before serving.

Boston Lettuce, Watercress and Mushroom Salad ●

Makes 4 servings

1 head Boston lettuce
½ cup packed watercress sprigs
4 mushrooms, sliced
  Herbed Vinaigrette Dressing
    (page 44)

Tear the lettuce into bite-size pieces and place in a serving bowl.

Coarsely chop the watercress and add it, along with the mushrooms, to the bowl.

Add enough dressing to moisten, and toss before serving.

Avocado and Cherry Tomato Salad ● ●

Colorful and elegant.

Makes 6 servings

1 avocado
1 pint cherry tomatoes
  Vinaigrette Dressing (page 44)
  watercress sprigs (garnish)

Halve and peel the avocado. Cut each half into six slices and arrange them in a fan shape on a serving plate.

Place the cherry tomatoes at the base of the fan. Spoon dressing over avocado and tomatoes, and garnish with watercress. Serve immediately, so the avocado does not discolor.

Salad Crunchies

For your next tossed salad, try these delicious, crunchy, garlic-flavored sunflower seeds. You can make them quickly. Just stir together ½ cup sunflower seeds, 1 teaspoon tamari and 1 garlic clove, minced, until the mixture is well combined. Place 1 tablespoon of corn oil in a heavy skillet, add the seeds and stir over low to medium heat until golden.

Greek Salad with Feta Cheese

This crumbly goat cheese is a classic complement for tomatoes and herbs.

Makes 4 servings

12 leaves romaine lettuce
 4 medium tomatoes
 2 medium cucumbers
½ cup crumbled feta cheese
 2 tablespoons minced fresh dill
 1 garlic clove
   Vinaigrette Dressing (page 44)
   parsley sprigs (garnish)

Arrange three romaine leaves on each of four serving plates. Cut the tomatoes into thin wedges and arrange on the lettuce.

Peel and chop the cucumbers and divide among the serving plates, lightly covering the tomatoes. Sprinkle some cheese over each salad.

Mix the dill and the garlic, pushed through a garlic press or minced, with the dressing. Drizzle each salad with some of the dressing and garnish with parsley sprigs.

NOTE: The entire salad can be arranged on a large plate and served at the table.

Orange–Tarragon Potato Salad ●

A perfect picnic potato salad, this contains no eggs or milk products that spoil easily.

Makes 6 servings

 6 cups cubed new potatoes
 8 scallions, sliced diagonally
 3 tablespoons sunflower oil
1½ tablespoons malt vinegar
 1 tablespoon minced fresh
      tarragon or 1 teaspoon dried
      tarragon

½ teaspoon grated orange rind
   dash of freshly grated nutmeg
      (optional)
   tarragon sprigs (garnish)
   orange peel twists (garnish)

Place potatoes in a large saucepan and cover with cold water; bring to a boil. Reduce heat, cover and simmer until the potatoes are firm-tender, about 10 to 15 minutes.

Add the scallions to the pan, turn off heat, cover the pan and let the vegetables sit for about a minute.

Combine the oil, vinegar, tarragon and orange rind to make a dressing. Drain the potatoes and scallions and place them in a large bowl.

Pour the dressing over the potatoes and dust with nutmeg, if desired. Toss until all the potatoes are coated with dressing.

Serve the salad either warm or chilled. Garnish with tarragon sprigs and orange peel twists.

Asparagus Salad with Pine Nuts ● ●

Makes 4 servings

 1 pound asparagus spears
 1 tablespoon olive oil
¼ cup pine nuts
 1 large garlic clove
 4 teaspoons tarragon vinegar
   Boston lettuce leaves
   dill sprigs (garnish)

Trim the tough ends from the asparagus and peel off a thin layer of skin up the scaled tips. Cut into 1½-inch lengths on the diagonal.

Steam the asparagus until firm-tender, then cool it under cold running water. Set aside. Refrigerate, if desired, until ready to serve.

To prepare the dressing, place the oil in a small skillet with the pine nuts and stir over low to medium heat just until the pine nuts begin to turn golden brown.

Remove from heat. Push the garlic through a garlic press into the hot pan and stir well, until the garlic is lightly cooked. Stir in vinegar. Allow to cool.

Just before serving, combine the asparagus and dressing in a small bowl. Toss well.

Place lettuce leaves in a serving bowl or on individual plates. Top with the asparagus. Garnish with dill and serve.

Pineapple–Date–Cabbage Salad ●

This unusual combo is sweet and crunchy.

Makes 6 servings

¼ ripe pineapple
3 carrots, shredded or thinly sliced
1 cup finely shredded cabbage
⅓ cup chopped dates
¼ cup sunflower seeds
¼ cup sunflower oil
2 tablespoons lemon juice
1 teaspoon honey
½ teaspoon grated lemon rind
    mint sprigs (garnish)

Peel the pineapple and remove the tough center core. Chop the pineapple into bite-size pieces. Reserve any liquid to add to the dressing.

Combine the pineapple, carrots, cabbage, dates and sunflower seeds in a large bowl.

To make the dressing, combine the pineapple liquid with the oil, lemon juice, honey and lemon rind in a small jar or bowl. Shake or stir until combined.

Pour the dressing over the salad. Toss well. Cover tightly and chill. Garnish with mint sprigs before serving.

Apple–Walnut Coleslaw ●

Makes 6 to 8 servings

4 cups shredded green cabbage
1 cup shredded red cabbage
2 tart red apples, cored and diced
½ cup chopped walnuts
2 tablespoons sunflower seeds
¼ cup buttermilk
2 tablespoons yogurt
2 tablespoons sunflower oil
1 tablespoon tarragon vinegar
1 teaspoon maple syrup
    dash of freshly grated nutmeg

Toss the cabbage, apples, walnuts and sunflower seeds together in a large serving bowl.

To make the dressing, combine the remaining ingredients in a small jar or bowl and shake or stir until well blended.

Pour the dressing over the cabbage mixture and toss. Cover tightly and chill before serving.

Cabbage–Grape–Pecan Salad ● ●

Makes 8 servings

6 cups shredded cabbage
1 cup red grapes, halved and seeded
1 large tart red apple, diced
3 tablespoons chopped pecans
    Poppy Seed Dressing (page 46)

Place the cabbage in a large serving bowl. Add the grapes, apples and pecans.

Add enough dressing to moisten the salad. Toss before serving.

NOTE: Any leftover salad should be refrigerated, tightly covered. It will keep well for 1 or 2 days.

Kidney Bean and Chick-Pea Salad ● ●

Makes 4 servings

1 cup cooked kidney beans
¾ cup cooked chick-peas
1 sweet red pepper, chopped
½ cup thinly sliced celery
3 scallions, chopped
3 tablespoons olive oil
2 tablespoons cider vinegar
½ teaspoon Dijon-style mustard
¼ teaspoon chili powder
1 teaspoon tamari
   minced fresh parsley (garnish)
1 cup cherry tomatoes (garnish)

In a serving bowl, toss together the kidney beans, chick-peas, peppers, celery and scallions.

To prepare the dressing, combine the oil, vinegar, mustard, chili powder and tamari in a cruet or a small jar with a lid. Shake well to combine.

Pour the dressing over the salad and toss well. Garnish with parsley and tomatoes. Chill before serving.

Beet and Carrot Salad with Ginger ● ●

Makes 8 servings

4 medium red beets
1 pound carrots
¼ cup lemon juice
2 tablespoons sunflower oil
2 tablespoons apple juice
1 tablespoon grated peeled ginger
   root
2 teaspoons honey
   dash of freshly grated nutmeg
4 cups coarsely shredded romaine
   lettuce or spinach leaves
1 cup Sour Yogurt-Cream (page 132)

Peel the beets and remove their tops. Shred the beets and carrots. (There should be about 4 cups.)

To make the dressing, combine the lemon juice, oil, apple juice, ginger, honey and nutmeg in a small bowl.

In a large bowl, toss together the vegetables and dressing. Chill overnight.

Arrange the lettuce or spinach around the edge of a round serving plate. Place a small bowl containing the sour yogurt-cream in the center of the plate.

Spoon the salad on top of the greens. Let guests serve themselves.

Lentil and Walnut Salad ● ●

You'll have a hard time finding a more delicious lentil salad!

Makes 4 servings

1 cup lentils
3 cups water
1 carrot
1 tablespoon tamari
10 sprigs parsley
¼ teaspoon whole cloves
1 garlic clove, peeled
½ cup chopped walnuts
2 tablespoons olive oil
2 tablespoons Sour Yogurt-Cream
      (page 132)
1 tablespoon minced shallots
⅛ teaspoon ground toasted cumin
      seeds
¼ cup minced fresh parsley
   red leaf lettuce
   red pepper rings (garnish)
   green pepper rings (garnish)

Place the lentils, water, carrot, tamari, parsley sprigs, cloves and garlic in a medium saucepan. Bring the water to a boil, reduce heat, cover and simmer just until tender, 25 to 30 minutes. Drain any liquid and remove the garlic clove, the carrot and as many parsley sprigs and cloves as you can find.

Place the walnuts in a small skillet with the oil. Saute just until the walnuts are a light golden brown. Remove from heat.

When the nuts have cooled, add the sour yogurt-cream, shallots, cumin and minced parsley and stir well until combined.

Gently fold the nut and parsley mixture into the lentils.

Arrange the lettuce on a serving plate. Spoon the salad on top of the leaves and garnish with red and green pepper rings. Serve with whole grain crackers and crisp raw vegetables.

NOTE: To toast cumin seeds, heat them in a small, dry cast-iron skillet until they release their aroma. To grind the toasted seeds, place them in a blender and process with short bursts at high speed until the seeds are finely ground.

Seasonal vegetables and dried beans can make winter salads exciting in their own right. Pictured left to right are Kidney Bean and Chick-Pea Salad, Beet and Carrot Salad with Ginger and Lentil and Walnut Salad.

Strawberry and Red Onion Salad ● ●

Makes 4 servings

16 leaves spinach or Bibb lettuce
  4 thin slices red onion
20 large strawberries
    Celery Seed Dressing (page 46)

Arrange the spinach or lettuce on individual serving plates. Separate the onion slices into rings and divide them among the plates.

    Arrange either whole or sliced berries over the onions. Drizzle the salad with dressing. Chill, if desired.

Variation: Serve with Strawberry-Garlic Mayonnaise (page 49) instead of celery seed dressing.

Zucchini and Pink Grapefruit Salad ●

This unusual salad presents a delicate rainbow of colors that leads to golden nutrition.

Makes 6 servings

1 to 2 pink grapefruits
2 to 3 small zucchinis
3 cups coarsely shredded spinach
  Honey-Lime Dressing (page 44)

Peel the grapefruit and remove any white membrane. Cut out grapefruit sections with a sharp knife, removing any membranes.

    Cut the zucchinis diagonally into thin slices.

    Arrange the salad on a flat, round serving plate, with the spinach around the outside, the grapefruit sections just inside the ring of spinach and the zucchini circling the center of the plate.

    Leave enough room to place a small bowl of dressing in the center of the plate. Cover tightly and chill, if desired.

Black Raspberry and Avocado Salad

● ●

Makes 4 servings

10 to 12 large leaves spinach, shredded
1 large avocado, peeled and thinly
     sliced
¾ cup black raspberries
     Honey-Lime Dressing (page 44)

Divide the spinach among individual
serving plates. Fan the avocado
slices over the spinach. Top each
salad with a small handful of berries.
     Moisten each portion with
dressing. Serve immediately.

Blueberry-Wheatberry Salad

● ● ●

Makes 4 servings

1 cup blueberries
1 cup cooked wheatberries
¼ cup finely chopped walnuts
¼ cup minced celery
¼ cup minced red onion
1 tablespoon minced fresh dill
     Honey-Lime Dressing (page 44)
     spinach leaves

Combine the blueberries, wheatberries,
walnuts, celery, onions and dill in a
medium bowl. Toss with dressing.
Serve on a bed of
spinach leaves.

Fruit and vegetable combinations make colorful salads with a unique taste. Try the Strawberry and Red Onion Salad (far left)—a surprising marriage of flavors! The Black Raspberry and Avocado Salad (above) is an exciting arrangement of colors and flavors. The Blueberry-Wheatberry Salad (below) is rare and hearty.

Dressings

Once you have assembled a colorful variety of greens and vegetables or fruit, you'll want to give them a finishing touch with an appropriate dressing. Making your own dressing takes just 2 minutes, and you can make it ahead and store it, tightly covered, in the refrigerator. Besides tasting better than anything you can buy, homemade dressings have no chemical stabilizers and additives so often found in commercial brands. Moreover, you can use polyunsaturated oils.

Vinaigrette Dressing ●

Makes ¾ cup

⅔ cup virgin olive oil
¼ cup lemon juice
2 teaspoons Dijon-style mustard
2 tablespoons minced shallots
1 tablespoon grated Parmesan
    cheese

Combine the ingredients in a small jar with a lid. Shake well until thoroughly combined.

Store in the refrigerator in a tightly covered container. Return to room temperature before using.

Variations: For *Minted Vinaigrette Dressing,* add 2 tablespoons minced fresh mint. For *Herbed Vinaigrette Dressing,* add 1 tablespoon minced fresh parsley, 2 teaspoons minced fresh thyme and 2 teaspoons minced fresh marjoram, or 1 teaspoon each of the dried herbs.

Tarragon-Yogurt Dressing ●

Makes 1½ cups

¼ cup tarragon vinegar
2 teaspoons Dijon-style mustard
1 egg yolk
½ cup sunflower oil
1 garlic clove

1 cup yogurt
1 tablespoon minced fresh
    tarragon or ¼ teaspoon
    dried tarragon

Place the vinegar, mustard and egg yolk in a blender and process on low speed until smooth.

With the blender running on medium speed, add the oil very slowly. When all of the oil is incorporated, add the garlic, pushed through a garlic press or minced, and the yogurt. Stir with a spatula until combined.

Honey-Lime Dressing ●

Makes ½ cup

3 tablespoons lime juice
1 tablespoon honey
½ teaspoon dry mustard
¼ teaspoon finely grated lemon or
    lime rind
⅛ teaspoon paprika
⅛ teaspoon ground coriander
1 egg yolk
½ cup sunflower oil

Place the lime juice, honey, mustard, lemon or lime rind, paprika, coriander and egg yolk in a blender. Process on low speed until combined.

With the blender running, add the oil in a slow, steady stream until it's all incorporated. Store in the refrigerator in a tightly covered container.

A trio of tasty dressings. Try Vinaigrette or Tarragon-Yogurt Dressing on green salads and Honey-Lime Dressing on combinations of fruit and greens.

Yogurt Dressing ●

Makes 2 cups

1 shallot, quartered
2 tablespoons rice vinegar
2 tablespoons lemon juice
1 teaspoon Dijon-style mustard
¼ teaspoon dry mustard
  dash of paprika
½ cup sunflower oil
1 cup yogurt

Place the shallot, vinegar, lemon juice, mustard, dry mustard and paprika in a blender. Process on low speed until smooth.

With the blender running on low speed, add the oil in a very slow, steady stream until it's all incorporated.

Add the yogurt and process on low speed until it's well mixed in, stopping to scrape down the sides as necessary.

NOTE: Rice vinegar is available in Oriental and health food stores.

Herbed Goddess Dressing ● ●

Similar to green goddess dressing, this tangy topping for fish, cooked broccoli or vegetable salads relies on yogurt instead of heavy sour cream, and forgoes the anchovies.

Makes ¾ cup

½ cup Whole-Egg Mayonnaise
    (page 48)
½ cup yogurt
2 tablespoons minced scallions
1½ tablespoons minced flatleaf
    parsley
1 teaspoon tarragon vinegar
1 teaspoon lemon juice
½ garlic clove, minced

Place the ingredients in a medium, wide-mouth jar. Stir until combined.

Store in the refrigerator in a tightly covered container. Use within 4 or 5 days.

Herbed Roquefort Dressing ● ●

Makes 1 cup

½ cup buttermilk
¼ cup Herbed Goddess Dressing
    (this page)
¼ cup crumbled Roquefort cheese

In a small bowl or pint jar with a lid, stir together the buttermilk and dressing. Add the cheese and stir just until combined.

Store in the refrigerator in a tightly covered container.

Celery Seed Dressing ●

Makes about ¾ cup

3 tablespoons tarragon vinegar
2 teaspoons honey
½ teaspoon dry mustard
½ teaspoon celery seeds
½ cup safflower oil

In a medium bowl, whisk together the vinegar, honey, mustard and celery seeds.

Add the oil slowly, whipping the dressing with the whisk to incorporate the oil.

Serve over fruit or a combination of fruit and salad greens.

Poppy Seed Dressing ●

Try this ever-so-slightly-sweet dressing on salads combining fruit and greens.

Makes ½ cup

½ cup sunflower oil
2 tablespoons lemon juice
1 teaspoon honey
1 teaspoon poppy seeds
¼ teaspoon ground coriander
⅛ teaspoon dry mustard

Place the ingredients in a small bowl and beat together with a small wire whisk or a spoon.

Store in the refrigerator in a tightly covered container.

Grapefruit Cup ● ●

Serve this salad in hollowed-out grapefruit halves set in bowls of crushed ice.

Makes 4 servings

2 pink grapefruits
1 apple, cubed
1 pear, cubed
½ cup seedless red grapes
3 tablespoons yogurt
2 teaspoons honey
  mint sprigs (garnish)

Cut the grapefruits in half crosswise. Cut the segments free with a sharp knife and place them in a medium bowl. Carefully pull the remaining membranes out of the grapefruit halves to make hollow cups.

Gently toss together the grapefruit sections, apple and pear cubes and grapes. Divide the fruit among the grapefruit cups. Chill, if desired.

In a small bowl, combine the yogurt and honey to make a dressing. Drizzle over the fruit just before serving. Garnish with mint sprigs.

Orange and Radish Salad with Minted Vinaigrette ●

Makes 4 servings

4 cups lightly packed spinach leaves
  or 2 small heads Boston
    lettuce, separated into leaves
2 large navel oranges
3 large red radishes
  Minted Vinaigrette Dressing
    (page 44)
¼ cup pine nuts or slivered almonds

Arrange the spinach or lettuce on individual plates or on a large serving platter.

Peel the oranges, removing the white membranes. Cut the fruit crosswise into thin slices. Thinly slice the radishes.

Arrange the oranges on the greens, overlapping the slices. Then arrange the radishes on top of the orange slices.

Drizzle the salad with dressing and sprinkle with pine nuts or almonds.

Fiddlehead Fern Salad ● ●

As an early spring salad, this is unmatched.

Makes 4 servings

20 to 24 fiddlehead ferns
¾ cup Vinaigrette Dressing (page 44)
1 head Boston lettuce, separated
    into leaves
2 tablespoons minced red onion
2 tablespoons feta cheese, finely
    crumbled

Steam the fiddlehead ferns just until crisp-tender, 4 to 5 minutes. Cool them under cold running water to prevent further cooking.

When the ferns are cool, place them in a medium bowl with the dressing. Cover tightly and refrigerate 6 hours or overnight.

Arrange lettuce on serving plates. Place some of the marinated fiddleheads on the lettuce.

Sprinkle each of the salads with some minced onion and cheese.

NOTE: Frozen fern heads are available in some areas.

Fiddlehead Ferns

In early spring, the tightly rolled fronds of fern plants look like the scrolls decorating the ends of tiny violins, hence the name "fiddleheads."

Ostrich ferns, which give rise to these delicate edible heads each spring, can be distinguished from other ferns in several ways. Their stems and fronds are smooth, not fuzzy. The fiddleheads are also smooth and covered with brown, papery scales.

Collect the fiddleheads when they are about 5 inches high and still tightly curled.

The best way to clean the ferns is to place them in a large pot of water and rub off the scales by hand, paying particular attention to those curled in the leafy tip. Rinse them well, then steam lightly for marinated salads or until firm-tender to serve as a vegetable. For a uniquely crunchy addition to a tossed salad, do not cook the fiddleheads at all.

Mayonnaise

Homemade mayonnaise has developed quite a mystique, but preparing it in a blender is really simple. Moreover, its taste is superior to any mayonnaise on the market. Even better, it's healthier. For example, it's made with highly unsaturated oil and contains no sugar or salt. Still, remember to use mayonnaise sparingly, for it is basically a mixture of egg and oil.

Whole-Egg Mayonnaise ●

Makes 1 cup

1 egg
1 tablespoon lemon juice
¼ teaspoon dry mustard
   dash of cayenne pepper
¾ cup sunflower oil
¼ cup olive oil

Place the egg, lemon juice, mustard and cayenne in a blender. Process on medium speed for 1 minute, or until the mixture is light and foamy.
   With the blender running, slowly add the oils. The first ¼ cup of oil should be added as a series of drops, then the remaining oil in a very thin stream.

Variation: Make a tangy yogurt mayonnaise by mixing equal parts of yogurt and whole-egg mayonnaise.

Herbed Mayonnaise ● ●

Makes 1 cup

1 cup water
2 tablespoons fresh tarragon
1 tablespoon fresh parsley
1 cup Whole-Egg Mayonnaise
   (this page)

Bring the water to a boil in a small saucepan. Add the herbs, then reduce heat and simmer for 1 minute.
   Drain the herbs well, then pat them dry.
   Finely chop the herbs and stir them into the mayonnaise. Store in the refrigerator in a tightly covered container.

Ricotta Mayonnaise ●

Makes ¾ cup

If you want to cut back on fat, this homemade mayonnaise is a tasty step in the right direction.

½ cup ricotta cheese
1 egg
1 tablespoon lemon juice
1 teaspoon sunflower oil
1 teaspoon Dijon-style mustard
   dash of cayenne pepper

Place the ingredients in a blender and process on medium speed until smooth.
   Store in the refrigerator in a tightly covered container.

Variation: For mayonnaise with more "bite," add one-half garlic clove to the blender with the other ingredients. (If you're brave, add a whole clove.)

Making Your Own Herb and Fruit Vinegars

Flavored vinegars add a low-calorie, low-sodium lift to salads and cooked vegetables or fruit.

Use herbs or berries to flavor basic cider vinegar. For herb vinegars, heat 2 cups cider vinegar in an enamel, glass or stainless steel pan until the vinegar is just below the boiling point. Rinse whole sprigs of tarragon, thyme, rosemary, savory, basil, oregano, marjoram or dill, then pat them dry. Place 2 or 3 sprigs of the desired herb in a decorative pint jar. (A peeled garlic clove can be added, if desired, but remove it after 2 days.) Pour in the hot vinegar, allow to cool, then cover and store in a cool, dark place.

For berry vinegar, add 1 tablespoon honey to each pint of vinegar as it is heated. Place 1 cup rinsed, dried berries in a pint jar. Add a small twist of orange peel, if desired. Pour the hot vinegar into the jar. Allow to cool to room temperature, then cover and let steep for 2 to 3 days. If the berries become soft and unattractive, they may be strained out through a double thickness of cheesecloth. The vinegar can be poured into smaller, decorative jars for gift-giving.

Garlic Mayonnaise ●

Makes 1 cup

3 tablespoons lemon juice
1 egg
1 garlic clove
½ cup sunflower oil
¼ cup virgin olive oil

Place the lemon juice, egg and garlic, pushed through a garlic press, in a blender. Process on medium speed at least 1 minute.

With the blender running on medium speed, add the oil a drop at a time for the first several tablespoons, then in a thin stream, until all the oil is incorporated and the mixture is a thick sauce. (The mayonnaise will not thicken properly if the oil is added too quickly.)

Variation: For *Strawberry-Garlic Mayonnaise,* add 8 to 10 strawberries just after the oil is blended. If you are presenting a buffet and would like to serve several sauces, remove half of the garlic mayonnaise from the blender and add 4 strawberries to the remaining mixture.

Eggless Tofu Mayonnaise ●

Makes 1 cup

¾ cup crumbled tofu
2 tablespoons cider vinegar
1 teaspoon Dijon-style mustard
1 teaspoon tamari
2 tablespoons sunflower oil

Combine the tofu, vinegar, mustard and tamari in a blender. Process on low speed until smooth.

With the blender running, slowly add the oil and continue blending until it is thoroughly incorporated.

Store in the refrigerator in a tightly covered container.

5

Soups and Stews

Soup is just the thing to start or *make* a meal. Economical stew is both versatile and delicious.

Say the word "soup" and the imagination conjures up a steaming bowl that warms both body and soul. Even better than the pleasure it brings, soup is nutritious. In fact, it's hard to find a more pleasant way to use so many healthful ingredients. And when you create your own low-salt stocks, you've doubled your investment in health. (Freeze any stock that you will not be using within a day or two. Stocks made without salt spoil more rapidly than salted ones.)

With soup, as with salad, you'll see seasonal variations. Bell Pepper Soup, Butternut Squash Soup and Cauliflower Soup are harvest favorites, for example. But you need not be bound by the seasons. If you have a garden, or even just access to a farm stand, Garden-Vegetable Chicken Stock is a rich (but fat-free and low-salt) basis for any dish. Prepare it when produce is plentiful, then freeze it in convenient quantities to enjoy on a day when the garden bears only a mantle of snow.

For a robust winter soup, you can choose from Black Bean, Paprika-Beef, or Lamb and Lentil Soup. Any one of them will provide the energy you need to tackle cold, icy days.

And when those winter days are only a dim memory—when the weather is, in fact, too hot to handle—cool off with a variety of colorful cold soups: Chilled Blueberry Soup, Strawberry-Melon Soup or tangy Gazpacho.

If you're a weight watcher, pay special attention to soup. It can help you take off pounds by curbing your appetite for richer fare. And if you're a vegetarian, simply substitute Tamari Stock for those made with meat. It turns many soups into vegetarian dishes, adding the heartiness of a beef stock without using any meat. For light but luscious vegetarian soups, substitute Vegetable Stock.

Fish Stock ● ●

Fish stock is superb as a base for fish or seafood soups and chowders and makes great poaching liquid for whole fish or fillets. When preparing stock, choose the trimmings of lean white fish such as cod, haddock, flounder, halibut, red snapper, sea bass and sole. Should your fishmonger fillet any of these fish for you, be sure to request the trimmings. In addition, fish dealers usually can sell trimmings separately.

Makes 1 quart

1 pound fish bones and heads (no gills)
4 cups cold water
2 tablespoons tarragon vinegar
1 stalk celery with leaves, quartered
1 carrot, cut into 2-inch pieces
1 small leek, halved
3 sprigs parsley
1 bay leaf

Place fish trimmings, water, vinegar, celery, carrots, leeks, parsley and bay leaf in a large saucepan. Heat to the boiling point, then reduce heat and simmer, uncovered, for 30 minutes.

Place a colander over a large bowl and line it with two layers of cheesecloth. Carefully strain the stock. Do not press the trimmings or squeeze the cloth.

Low-Sodium Chicken Stock ● ●

Makes 3 quarts

3 to 4 pounds chicken backs and
    wings
2 carrots, halved
2 stalks celery, halved
1 large onion, halved
3 to 4 sprigs parsley
1 tablespoon lemon juice
⅛ teaspoon dried thyme
1 bay leaf
2 peppercorns
14 cups water

Place the ingredients in a large kettle or stockpot. Bring to a boil and skim off any foam that rises to the surface.

Reduce heat, cover and simmer for about 2½ hours.

Place a colander over a large bowl and line it with two layers of cheesecloth. Carefully strain the stock.

Chill the strained stock. Remove any solidified fat from the surface before using.

NOTE: Refrigerated, this stock will keep for 3 to 4 days. Frozen, it will keep for 2 to 3 months. (Freeze in pint or quart containers for convenience.)

Vegetable Stock ● ●

Substitute this flavorful stock for chicken or beef stock if you want a wholly vegetarian dish.

Makes 1 quart

2 onions, quartered
2 carrots, thickly sliced
2 stalks celery, halved
1 leek, coarsely chopped
1 sweet red pepper, quartered
2 mushrooms, quartered
1 small tomato, seeded and coarsely
     chopped
4 garlic cloves, peeled
1 bay leaf
1 peppercorn
5 cups water

Place the ingredients in a stockpot or kettle and set over high heat. Bring to a boil, then cover, reduce heat and simmer 1 hour.
    Place a colander over a large bowl. Line it with two layers of cheesecloth and strain the stock. Refrigerate or freeze, covered.

NOTE: Refrigerated, the stock will keep 2 to 3 days. (Freeze in cup or pint containers for convenience.)
    Save vegetable trimmings in a bag in the freezer to use in making stocks. Avoid cabbage, cauliflower, broccoli or brussels sprouts because of their overpowering flavor.

Variation: Substitute 6 to 8 scallions, halved, for the leek.

Garden-Vegetable Chicken Stock ● ●

Stock up when garden produce is plentiful. Your soups will be the richer for it.

Makes 2 quarts

8 cups water
4 onions, quartered
3 stalks celery, chopped
6 carrots, sliced
6 scallions, halved
1 tomato, chopped
3 sprigs parsley
3 chicken backs
3 chicken necks

Place the ingredients in a large kettle or stockpot. Bring to a boil and skim off any foam that rises to the surface.
    Reduce heat, cover and simmer for about 2 hours.
    Place a colander over a large bowl and line it with two layers of cheesecloth. Strain the stock.
    Chill the strained stock. Remove any solidified fat from the surface before using.

Tamari Stock ●

This meatless broth is an excellent substitute for beef stock. An unusual ingredient, blackstrap molasses, adds a rich flavor to the stock.

Makes 2 cups

2 cups water
2 tablespoons tamari
⅛ teaspoon blackstrap molasses

Place the ingredients in a small saucepan. Heat through and serve as a plain soup. Or stir together until the molasses is dissolved. Use in any recipe calling for beef stock.

Bell Pepper Soup ●

An excellent soup; the recipe can easily be doubled.

Makes 4 servings

2 cups chopped sweet red peppers
1 leek, finely chopped
1½ tablespoons corn oil
2½ cups Low-Sodium Chicken Stock
 (page 52)
 sweet red pepper rings (garnish)
 minced fresh parsley (garnish)

Place the peppers and leeks in a large saucepan with the oil. Cover and cook over low to medium heat for 8 to 10 minutes, stirring occasionally.

Add the stock. Bring to a boil, then reduce heat and simmer for 15 minutes. Remove from heat.

Place half of the mixture in a blender. Process on low speed until smooth. Return blended mixture to the saucepan and heat through before serving.

To serve, place soup in a tureen or individual serving bowls. Float pepper rings on top of the soup and sprinkle with a bit of parsley.

NOTE: This soup also can be chilled before serving for hot-weather meals.

French-Style Onion Soup ● ●

An attractive dish to set before anyone!

Makes 4 servings

4 large sweet Spanish onions
2 teaspoons olive oil
1 tablespoon whole wheat flour
1 garlic clove, minced
4 cups Low-Sodium Chicken Stock
 (page 52)
2 tablespoons tamari
½ teaspoon blackstrap molasses
4 slices whole wheat toast
1 cup shredded Swiss or Gruyere
 cheese

Cut the onions in half lengthwise, then cut into thin half-circles. Heat the oil in a very large skillet or large flameproof casserole. Add the onions, cover the pan, and cook slowly over low heat. Stir occasionally. Add a few drops of water, if needed, to prevent the onions from scorching.

When the onions are tender and begin to turn golden brown, sprinkle on the flour and add the garlic. Stir until onions are coated with flour. Cook, stirring constantly, for 2 to 3 minutes.

Add the stock, tamari and molasses. Cover and cook about 15 minutes over low heat.

To serve, divide the soup among four ovenproof serving bowls. Top each serving with a slice of whole wheat toast trimmed to fit the bowl. Sprinkle with cheese and place in a preheated 400°F oven or under a broiler until the cheese is melted and golden brown. Serve immediately.

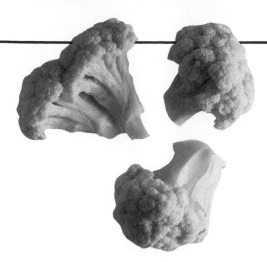

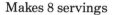

Cauliflower Soup ● ●

Colorful vegetables float in a creamy soup livened up with cheese.

Makes 8 servings

1 sweet Spanish onion, finely
    chopped
2 tablespoons sunflower oil
2 tablespoons whole wheat flour
¼ teaspoon dried thyme
12 cups coarsely chopped cauliflower
    (2 large heads)
4 to 5 cups Low-Sodium Chicken
    Stock (page 52) or Vegetable
    Stock (page 53)
2 cups skim milk
2 cups thinly sliced carrots
1 sweet red pepper, finely chopped
1 cup shredded sharp cheddar cheese
2 tablespoons minced fresh parsley
  dash of ground nutmeg

Place the onions and oil in a large, heavy-bottom stockpot or kettle. Stir over medium heat until the onions are slightly tender. Stir in the flour and thyme.

Add the cauliflower, 4 cups of stock and milk. Bring to a boil, then reduce heat and simmer for 15 minutes.

Remove half of the cauliflower and place in a blender. Process on medium speed until smooth. Return the blended mixture to the pot.

Add the carrots and peppers. Return to a boil, then reduce heat, partially cover and simmer for another 20 minutes.

Stir in the cheese, parsley and nutmeg. Add some additional stock if the soup is too thick. Serve hot.

Butternut Squash Soup ● ●

Makes 6 servings

1 tablespoon butter
1 tablespoon whole wheat flour
3 cups butternut squash puree
2 cups milk
1 cup light cream
1 tablespoon maple syrup
½ teaspoon ground cinnamon
⅛ teaspoon ground cloves
2 oranges

Melt the butter in a large, heavy-bottom saucepan over low heat.

Stir in the flour. Cook over low heat, stirring constantly, for 1 to 2 minutes.

Stir in the squash puree, then add the milk, cream, syrup, cinnamon and cloves. Bring just to the boiling point, then turn off heat and cover the pan.

Cut three thin slices from the middle of each orange and set aside for garnish. Squeeze the remaining oranges and add the juice to the soup.

To serve, ladle soup into individual bowls and float an orange slice in each bowl.

NOTE: To make butternut squash puree, cut two medium squash (about 4 pounds total) into cubes. (There should be 10 cups.) Steam the squash just until tender, then allow to cool and remove the skin. Place one batch of squash in a blender and process on low speed until smooth. Repeat until all the squash is pureed. The puree should be the consistency of applesauce. Simmer the puree in a large saucepan until it reaches the desired consistency; the final yield will be 3 to 4 cups.

Paprika-Beef Soup

Vegetable-thickened broth adds to the flavor of this richly satisfying soup.

Makes 8 servings

¼ cup corn oil
 1 pound beef chuck or round, cut
      into bite-size cubes
 2 medium onions, finely chopped
 8 cups water
 2 cups shredded carrots
 5 garlic cloves, minced
 3 tablespoons tomato paste
 3 tablespoons paprika
½ teaspoon caraway seeds
 1 tablespoon fresh marjoram or
      1½ teaspoons dried marjoram
 1 teaspoon grated lemon rind
 1 teaspoon light unsulfured molasses
      dash of cayenne pepper
 3 small potatoes, diced
 3 tablespoons tamari

In a stockpot or kettle, heat the oil over high heat until hot but not smoking. Dry the beef cubes by patting with paper towels, then add them to the hot oil.

A taste of New England anywhere you live—wholesome Fish Chowder.

Stir the beef cubes as they cook, until they're browned on all sides. Add the onions and a small amount of water, if needed, to prevent scorching. Cook until the onions are translucent.

Add the remaining water, carrots, garlic, tomato paste, paprika, caraway seeds, marjoram, lemon rind, molasses and cayenne. Bring to a boil over high heat, then stir well, reduce heat and cover. Simmer for 1½ to 2 hours, stirring occasionally.

Stir in the potatoes. Cover and simmer until the potatoes are tender, 10 to 15 minutes. Skim off any fat on the surface of the soup. Stir in the tamari and serve.

Fish Chowder ●

Makes 4 servings

¾ pound tilefish fillets
⅓ cup sliced scallions
 1 tablespoon olive oil
 1 teaspoon butter
 1 teaspoon minced garlic
 1 cup chopped tomatoes (with juice)
 3 cups Fish Stock or Low-Sodium
      Chicken Stock (page 52)
 1 cup cubed red potatoes
 2 teaspoons grated horseradish
 2 teaspoons lemon juice
½ teaspoon dried thyme
 2 bay leaves
      dash of cayenne pepper
 2 teaspoons minced fresh parsley
 1 teaspoon tamari

Cut the fish fillets into bite-size pieces. Set aside.

Cook the scallions in the oil and butter in a large saucepan over medium heat until they're limp. Add the garlic and stir another minute.

Add the tomatoes, stock, potatoes, horseradish, lemon juice, thyme, bay leaves and cayenne. Bring to a boil, then reduce heat and simmer for 15 minutes.

Add the fish and simmer an additional 5 minutes. Remove from heat and stir in the parsley and tamari. Remove bay leaves before serving. Serve hot.

Variation: Use haddock or perch fillets if tilefish is unavailable.

Lamb and Lentil Soup

Makes 8 servings

1 cup dried lentils
8 cups water
1 onion, chopped
2 garlic cloves, minced
½ sweet red pepper, chopped
1 stalk celery, sliced diagonally
4 carrots, sliced diagonally
¼ teaspoon dried tarragon
¼ teaspoon dried marjoram
¼ teaspoon ground allspice
⅛ teaspoon dried thyme
⅛ teaspoon ground cloves
⅛ teaspoon cayenne pepper
½ pound cooked lamb
⅔ cup tomato paste
2 tomatoes, peeled and coarsely chopped

Rinse the lentils and place them in a large pot. Add the water, onions, garlic, peppers, celery, carrots, herbs and spices. Bring to a boil, reduce heat, cover and simmer 45 minutes.

Chop the meat into bite-size pieces. Add to the pot, along with the tomato paste and tomatoes. Bring to a boil, then reduce heat and simmer an additional 30 minutes.

Variation: Substitute cooked beef or turkey dark meat for the lamb. Serve over cooked, lightly mashed potatoes.

Chicken Alphabet Soup ●

Children love to hunt for the letters in their names. You'll love seeing them eat such a nutritious bowl of tasty soup!

Makes 4 servings

1 chicken breast, halved
6 cups water
1 large carrot, cut into large pieces
1 large onion, sliced
½ stalk celery, quartered
1 bay leaf
1 garlic clove, halved
1 whole clove

1 carrot, thinly sliced on the diagonal
1 small onion, finely chopped
½ cup whole wheat alphabet noodles
2 tablespoons minced fresh parsley
1 teaspoon tamari

Place the chicken, water, large carrot pieces, sliced onion, celery, bay leaf, garlic and clove in a large saucepan. Bring to a boil and skim off any foam that rises to the surface.

Reduce heat, cover and simmer for 1 hour. Remove both halves of the chicken breast from the pan. Set one half aside for another use. Remove the meat from the remaining piece of chicken, chop it, and set aside.

Strain the stock. Remove the fat with a bulb baster or by chilling the stock and later removing the solidified fat. (In this case, refrigerate the chicken meat, too.)

Place the defatted stock with the chopped chicken meat in a large saucepan and bring to a boil. Cover, reduce heat and simmer for 20 minutes.

Add the sliced carrot, chopped onion and the alphabet noodles. Simmer an additional 20 minutes. Stir in the parsley and tamari. Serve hot.

NOTE: You can prepare this soup ahead up to the point of straining the stock. Refrigerate overnight to solidify fat. Remove fat and proceed with recipe.

Variation: Substitute ½ cup small whole wheat shells or whole wheat elbow macaroni for the alphabet noodles. Add them about 10 minutes before the soup is completed.

Bones in Stocks

By adding bones when you make stock, you also can add a significant amount of valuable calcium to these soup bases. To release the calcium from the bones, add a teaspoon or two of lemon juice to the stockpot, or add 1 or 2 tomatoes. The acid in these ingredients does the trick. Stock made in this manner may have as much as 125 milligrams of extra calcium in each cup, or as much as you'll find in ⅔ cup of cottage cheese.

Dutch Pea Soup ●

The British are noted for their damp, chilly fogs that are as "thick as pea soup." The Dutch climate doesn't differ much, alas, but the residents there comfort themselves with this hearty dish, fit for a meal!

Makes 8 servings

1 large leek, finely chopped
1 sweet Spanish onion, finely chopped
1 cup finely chopped celery
2 tablespoons corn oil
2 tablespoons butter
2 cups dried green split peas
1 garlic clove, minced
6 to 6½ cups water
2 tablespoons chopped fresh parsley
2 large potatoes, peeled and cubed
1 to 2 tablespoons tamari

Place the leeks, onions, celery, oil and butter in a large saucepan or pot. Cook over low to medium heat until the onions are translucent.

Stir in the peas until they are well mixed with the other vegetables. Add the garlic and stir well to combine.

Add 6 cups of water. Stir well to loosen any vegetables clinging to the bottom of the pan. Bring to a boil, then reduce heat, cover and simmer for 30 minutes.

Add the parsley and potatoes. Simmer an additional 30 to 40 minutes, until the potatoes are tender and the peas are mushy. (If the soup becomes too thick during the first 30 minutes of cooking, add an additional ½ cup of water.) Stir in tamari to taste, and serve hot.

NOTE: This soup may thicken as it cools. If so, add a little water when reheating any leftovers.

Variation: This is a vegetarian version of the traditional Dutch soup. If you'd like a meaty flavor, add a beef soup bone to the pot with the water. If there's any meat on the bone, chop it and add to the finished soup.

Lentil and Vegetable Soup ● ●

Makes 8 servings

7 cups water
1 cup dried lentils
¼ cup uncooked brown rice
5 to 6 carrots
3 tomatoes, peeled and chopped
2 onions, finely chopped
½ sweet red pepper, finely chopped
1 cup corn kernels
5 garlic cloves, minced
3 tablespoons tamari
2 tablespoons sunflower oil
1 tablespoon tomato paste
1 small zucchini
2 tablespoons minced fresh parsley

Place the water, lentils and rice in a large saucepan over medium heat. Cut the carrots diagonally into thick slices (there should be about 3 cups) and add to the lentils and rice.

Add the tomatoes, onions, peppers, corn, garlic, tamari, oil and tomato paste. Bring to a boil, then reduce heat, cover and simmer for 35 minutes.

Halve the zucchini. Remove the seeds and, if desired, set them aside for another use. Cut the outer part of the zucchini into 1½-inch julienne strips.

Add the zucchini to the pan and simmer another 10 minutes. Stir in the parsley and serve.

Black Bean Soup ●●

With colorful accompaniments, black bean soup makes a hearty main dish.

Makes 8 servings

1 pound dried black turtle beans
8 cups water
2 medium onions, finely chopped
¼ cup sunflower oil
2 to 3 garlic cloves, minced
2 bay leaves
½ teaspoon ground ginger
3 tablespoons tamari
2 tablespoons balsamic vinegar or
    red wine vinegar
2 cups hot cooked brown rice
1 cup chopped onions
1 cup chopped tomatoes

Soak the beans overnight in enough water to cover generously. Drain.

Place the beans with 8 cups of water in a large saucepan or pot. Cook over medium heat.

In a medium skillet, cook the onions in the oil until they begin to turn golden brown. Add the garlic and stir another minute or two.

Stir the onions, bay leaves and ginger into the beans. Bring the mixture to a boil, then reduce heat, cover and simmer for 2 hours.

Stir in the tamari and vinegar and cook another 30 to 40 minutes,

or until the beans are very tender and the soup has thickened slightly. Remove bay leaves.

To serve, ladle soup into a tureen. Place the rice, onions and tomatoes in separate serving bowls and let each person add them to the soup to taste. Serve with crusty bread and a green salad.

NOTE: Balsamic vinegar, made with basil, is available in the "gourmet" section of some supermarkets or in gourmet shops.

Yellow Split-Pea Soup ●

Makes 8 servings

7 cups water
2 cups dried yellow split peas
2 carrots, sliced
1 large onion, chopped
1 stalk celery, sliced
2 tomatoes, peeled and chopped
4 garlic cloves, minced
2 tablespoons sunflower oil
2 tablespoons tamari
1 sweet potato, diced

Place the water, peas, carrots, onions, celery, tomatoes, garlic, oil and tamari in a large, heavy-bottom saucepan. Bring to a boil.

Reduce heat, partially cover and simmer for 30 minutes. Add the sweet potato, cover and simmer another 30 minutes. Serve hot.

Vegetable Soup with Fennel ● ●

Makes 10 servings

3 large ripe tomatoes, peeled, seeded
    and coarsely chopped
4 carrots, sliced diagonally
½ stalk celery, sliced diagonally
1 medium sweet Spanish onion,
    chopped
1 small fennel bulb, chopped
1 cup corn kernels
⅓ cup barley
6 garlic cloves, thinly sliced
3 tablespoons minced fresh parsley
6 cups water
½ cup tomato paste
1 cup peas (fresh or frozen)
1 cup packed spinach leaves, thinly
    sliced
1 tablespoon minced fresh dill
2 teaspoons fresh tarragon or
    ½ teaspoon dried tarragon
2 tablespoons tamari
  fennel sprigs (garnish)

Place the tomatoes, carrots, celery, onions, chopped fennel, corn, barley, garlic, parsley and water in a kettle or stockpot. Bring to a boil, then reduce heat, cover and simmer for 1¼ hours.

    Add the tomato paste. (If using fresh peas, add them now and cook 10 minutes. If using frozen peas, add them during the final 5 minutes of cooking.) Add the spinach, dill and tarragon and cook 5 minutes longer. Stir in the tamari.

    Serve hot, garnished with fennel.

Variation: Other fresh herbs may be substituted for fennel.

Vegetable-Barley Soup

Makes 10 servings

8 cups water
4 cups sliced carrots
1 leek, chopped
1 stalk celery, chopped
5 garlic cloves, sliced
1½ cups shredded cabbage
½ cup chopped kale .
2 tomatoes, peeled, seeded and
    chopped
¼ cup barley
3 tablespoons olive oil
1 bay leaf
1 tablespoon minced fresh
    tarragon or ½ teaspoon dried
    tarragon
1 tablespoon minced fresh lovage or
    celery leaves
⅛ teaspoon ground allspice
2 tablespoons tamari
  fresh kale leaves (garnish)
  carrot curls (garnish)

Vegetable-Barley Soup rewards the palate with a richly varied combination of ingredients: cabbage, garlic, celery, leek, kale and herbs. Serve with whole grain popovers.

Place the water, carrots, leeks, celery, garlic, cabbage, kale, tomatoes, barley, oil, bay leaf, tarragon, lovage or celery leaves and allspice in a large kettle or stockpot.

Bring to a boil. Reduce heat, cover and simmer for 2 hours, stirring occasionally, until the flavors are well blended and the vegetables are very tender.

Remove bay leaf and stir in tamari before serving. Garnish with kale leaves and carrot curls.

Broccoli and Cheddar Soup ● ● ●

An elegant combination loaded with protein and calcium.

Makes 6 servings

    2 tablespoons sunflower oil
    2 tablespoons butter
1½ cups chopped onions
    1 bay leaf
    1 teaspoon fresh thyme or
        ¼ teaspoon dried thyme
    1 tablespoon whole wheat flour
    1 tablespoon unbleached flour
    4 cups chopped broccoli stalks,
        leaves and florets
2½ cups Low-Sodium Chicken Stock
        (page 52)
        dash of ground allspice
2½ cups thinly sliced broccoli florets
1½ cups milk
    2 cups packed shredded cheddar
        cheese
    2 tablespoons minced fresh parsley
        minced, unsalted pistachios
        (garnish)

Place the oil and butter in a large saucepan. When the butter has melted, add the onions, bay leaf and thyme. Stir over medium heat until the onions are tender, but not browned. Add the flours and stir to coat the onions.

Add the chopped broccoli, stock and allspice. Bring to a boil, then reduce heat, cover and simmer for about 8 minutes. The broccoli should be tender, but still bright green.

While the soup is cooking, steam the sliced broccoli florets for 7 to 8 minutes, until firm-tender and still bright green.

Remove the bay leaf from the soup. Place half of the soup in a blender with half of the milk. Process on low, then medium speed until very smooth. Repeat with the remaining soup and milk. Return the blended soup to the pan.

Add the cheese and stir over low heat until the cheese has melted. Add the steamed broccoli and the parsley. Heat through and serve, garnished with pistachios.

Cream of Vegetable Soup ●

The mellow blend of vegetables in this thick and hearty soup makes chilly weather worth waiting for.

Makes 6 servings

    4 cups Low-Sodium Chicken Stock
        (page 52)
    4 cups diced peeled potatoes
2½ cups diced peeled kohlrabi
    3 tablespoons butter
    1 large leek, finely chopped
    1 medium onion, finely chopped
    ¾ cup light cream
    ¾ cup milk
        snipped chives (garnish)

Place the stock, potatoes and kohlrabi in a large saucepan. Bring to a boil over medium heat, then reduce heat, cover and simmer.

Melt the butter in a medium skillet. Add the leeks and onions. Cook over low to medium heat until they are limp. Add to the soup.

Simmer for 40 to 45 minutes, or until the vegetables are all quite tender.

Place about one-third of the soup in a blender with the cream and milk. Process on low speed until smooth. Return the blended mixture to the pan.

Heat the soup through and garnish with chives before serving.

When to Add Herbs

Fresh herbs, such as minced parsley, dill or chives, are delicate. For that reason, add them near the end of the cooking time when preparing soups. The herbs will retain their delicate flavor and bright color if the soup is removed from the heat as soon as the herbs have wilted. Add dried herbs and stronger-flavored fresh herbs at the beginning of cooking. Crumbling dried herbs between your fingers will help release their flavor and aroma.

Smoky Eggplant Soup ● ●

Pimiento and eggplant, specially prepared, give the smoky flavor to this unique soup.

Makes 4 to 6 servings

½ cup dried baby lima beans
1 sweet red pepper
1 medium eggplant
1 leek
6 cups Low-Sodium Chicken Stock
    (page 52)
1 tablespoon Butter-Half (page 133)
2 tablespoons tamari
    dash of ground allspice
    minced fresh parsley (garnish)

Cover the lima beans with a generous amount of water and soak overnight. Drain the beans.

Place the pepper under a broiler or over a gas burner turned low. Keep turning the pepper until it is charred and the skin begins to bubble. (The pepper will be rather soft.) Wrap in a wet paper towel for 10 minutes.

Place the eggplant under a broiler or in a preheated 450°F oven. Cook, turning occasionally, until the outside is charred and the eggplant is soft.

Cut open the eggplant and scoop out the pulp into a medium bowl. Discard any seeds that are easily separated from the pulp.

Unwrap the pepper and separate the charred skin from the flesh, using a damp paper towel. (Do not place the pepper under running water or you'll lose much of the flavor.) Remove the seeds and stem and discard them.

Coarsely chop the eggplant and dice the pepper. Set aside.

Using a sharp knife, cut the leek in half, leaving about 2 inches of the white bottom intact. Spread the leek open under running water to remove all bits of sand and grit from the tops. Chop the leek finely.

Place the beans and stock in a large saucepan. Bring to a boil, then reduce heat, cover and simmer for 30 minutes.

Melt the butter-half in a medium skillet. Cook the leeks until lightly browned, adding a few drops of water, if necessary, to prevent scorching. Remove from heat.

Add the leeks, eggplant and pepper to the beans. Return to a boil, then reduce heat, cover and simmer about an hour longer, until the beans are tender.

Stir in the tamari and allspice. Serve garnished with parsley.

Chicken and Barley Stew ●

A simple dish, but good and hearty.

Makes 4 servings

4 chicken thighs, skinned
½ cup barley
5½ cups Low-Sodium Chicken Stock
    (page 52)
1 stalk celery, chopped
3 small carrots, sliced
1 large tomato, peeled and chopped
2 garlic cloves, minced
1 tablespoon tamari
½ teaspoon dried basil
⅛ teaspoon dried oregano
⅛ teaspoon dried thyme
    dash of cayenne pepper
2 tablespoons minced fresh parsley

Place the chicken, barley, stock, celery, carrots, tomatoes, garlic, tamari, herbs and cayenne in a large saucepan. Bring to a boil, then reduce heat and cover the pan. Simmer for 1¼ hours, stirring occasionally.

Remove the chicken from the pan and allow to cool slightly. Remove the meat from the bones and cut into bite-size pieces. Return the meat to the pan.

Simmer another 15 minutes, then stir in the parsley. Serve hot.

Lamb Stew with Chick-Peas ●

This stew is a variation on many Middle Eastern themes.

Makes 10 servings

1 cup dried chick-peas
1 pound lean lamb cubes
5 cups water
1 strip lemon rind
1 large onion, finely chopped
3 tablespoons olive oil
4 cups chopped peeled tomatoes
2 cups thickly sliced carrots
3 garlic cloves, minced
½ teaspoon freshly ground black
    pepper
½ teaspoon ground turmeric
½ teaspoon ground cumin
½ teaspoon paprika
¼ teaspoon ground coriander
¼ teaspoon freshly grated nutmeg
    dash of ground cardamom
3 tablespoons tamari
3 tablespoons minced fresh parsley

Cover the chick-peas with a generous amount of water and soak overnight. Drain and set aside.

Place the lamb and 5 cups of water in a large saucepan or pot. Add the lemon rind. Bring the water to a boil over low to medium heat and skim off any foam that rises to the surface.

While the lamb is cooking, place the onions and oil in a medium skillet. Cook over medium heat until the onions are translucent and slightly tender.

Remove the lemon rind from the pot. Add the onions, tomatoes, carrots, garlic, herbs and spices.

Bring the stew to a boil. Then reduce heat, cover and simmer, stirring occasionally, for 1½ to 2 hours, until the lamb is quite tender.

Stir in the tamari and parsley. Serve hot.

NOTE: This stew is wonderful served over hot cooked brown rice, whole grain noodles or mashed or chopped potatoes. You can freeze any leftovers for future quick meals.

Chicken Stew with Fennel ●

Makes 8 servings

3 tablespoons olive oil
4 chicken legs and thighs, skinned
6 cups Garden-Vegetable Chicken
    Stock (page 53)
2 tablespoons butter
1 onion, finely chopped
5 carrots, diced
1 cup diced celery root
1 fennel bulb, chopped
3 garlic cloves, minced
4 tomatoes, peeled, seeded and
    chopped
¼ teaspoon saffron threads
¼ cup minced fresh parsley

Heat the oil in a large, heavy-bottom saucepan or pot over medium heat. Add the chicken and brown the pieces.

Add the stock and bring it to a boil. Then reduce heat and cover the pan.

Melt the butter in a medium skillet. Add the onions and stir until lightly golden. Add the carrots, celery root, fennel and garlic. Stir about 5 minutes over low heat. Add the tomatoes, cover and cook for 10 minutes.

Add the cooked vegetables, saffron and parsley to the simmering stock. Cover and simmer for 1 hour.

When the meat is tender, remove the chicken pieces from the stew. Remove the meat from the bones, chop coarsely, and return to the pot. Heat through and serve.

Cold Soups

For a wonderful change of pace, prepare some delicate cold soup for dinner. Very European and very elegant, these soups are just the thing for a hot summer evening.

Choose Strawberry-Melon Soup and savor the special sweetness of this fruity blend of flavors, or let your eyes feast on the rich color of Chilled Blueberry Soup. Be tempted by the tang of Gazpacho, or blend a splendid peach puree to serve as a soup.

tips halfway to the caps and slip over the edge of the bowls.

Variation: Press the chilled soup through a strainer and serve over ice for a refreshing summer beverage.

Chilled Blueberry Soup ● ●

Makes 4 servings

2 cups blueberries
¾ cup apple juice
¼ cup orange juice
1 drop lemon extract
   dash of freshly grated nutmeg
4 thin orange slices (garnish)
¼ cup yogurt (garnish)

Place the blueberries, fruit juices and lemon extract in a small saucepan. Bring to a boil over medium heat, stirring occasionally.

Reduce heat and simmer for about 1 minute. Add nutmeg.

Pour the soup into a blender and process on low to medium speed until smooth. Chill the soup in the blender container or in individual serving bowls.

Float an orange slice on top of each serving and place a dollop of yogurt on each orange slice.

Strawberry–Melon Soup ● ●

Makes 4 servings

½ cantaloupe, cubed
1 cup apple juice
2 to 3 strawberries, halved
¼ teaspoon ground cardamom
   whole strawberries with caps
   (garnish)

Place the cantaloupe in a blender with the apple juice, strawberry halves and cardamom. Process on low, then medium speed until smooth.

Chill the soup in the blender container. Process again on medium speed before serving.

Pour the soup into four bowls. Slit the whole strawberries from their

Gazpacho ●

A traditional Spanish soup that is served chilled.

Makes 4 servings

  1 small onion, quartered
  1 large tomato, quartered
  1 sweet red pepper, seeded and
    quartered
1½ cups water
  ¼ cup tomato paste
  2 tablespoons olive oil
  2 tablespoons lemon juice
  1 garlic clove
  ⅛ teaspoon cayenne pepper
  1 cup finely chopped mushrooms
  1 stalk celery, finely chopped
  1 small cucumber, peeled, seeded
    and finely chopped
  1 tablespoon minced fresh parsley
  1 teaspoon minced fresh chives

Place the onions, tomato, pepper, water, tomato paste, oil, lemon juice, garlic and cayenne in a blender.

Process on medium speed until smooth, stopping to scrape down the sides as necessary. Pour into four serving bowls.

Divide the mushrooms, celery, cucumber, parsley and chives evenly among the bowls. Chill.

Summer Peach Soup ● ●

This quick and delicious soup is a perfect way to use those very ripe peaches that are nearly too soft to eat out of hand.

Makes 2 servings

3 to 4 large very ripe
    peaches
  mint sprigs (garnish)

Wash the peaches. Remove the pits and any bruised spots, but do not peel. Chop coarsely.

Place the peaches in a blender. Process on low speed until quite smooth. Serve chilled, garnished with mint sprigs.

Variation: Add a dollop of yogurt when serving. If peaches are not exceptionally flavorful, add 1 teaspoon of honey and a dash of lemon juice.

Appetizing Selections

Hors d'oeuvres are more than a snack. They can be nutritious and complement your special meals.

Hors d'oeuvres can play a supporting role by setting the tone for a meal or they can perform solo at a party. More than just something to nibble on, they can become tiny nuggets of nutrition. Either way, these star appetizers can enhance your healthy lifestyle, provided you bypass the usual, boring hors d'oeuvres—the nuts, the dip made from soup mix and fattening sour cream.

Instead, to introduce an elegant dinner, look to Minted Grapefruit Sections served in a stemmed goblet. Or set the stage with a stunning arrangement of fruit, which guests dip into a tangy combination of cottage cheese, yogurt and fruit juice, with just a hint of curry to add interest. You will be applauded for your ingenuity and culinary skill, and thanked—especially by the health-conscious—for your thoughtfulness.

For a little excitement, go Middle Eastern. Tabbouleh-Stuffed Mushrooms make this Lebanese salad stand-up party fare. Try Hummus Tahini, a chick-pea and sesame dip that tastes terrific with pita bread or raw vegetable sticks. Spinach Triangles are fabulous, too. Your party will draw rave reviews.

Mexican food buffs will have a fiesta with Guacamole, Mexican Bean Dip and a Nachos Platter! All of these add fiber, and the avocado provides some potassium and vitamin C as well.

On those extra-special occasions when you have a large gathering, make a Camembert Torte. It's an unusual, sensuously rich offering. It's so beautiful, in fact, that it serves as a centerpiece for the entire buffet table, and will earn you a free round of applause.

Appetizers and hors d'oeuvres are more than salty tidbits to serve with cocktails. They can be a fascinating and healthful overture to any meal. (Recipes have been evaluated for nutrition per serving.)

Fruit Pinwheel ● ●

Makes 10 servings

½ lemon
1 ripe pineapple, peeled and cored
2 kiwi fruits
2 nectarines
¼ honeydew melon
2 pears
2 pints strawberries
1 bunch large red grapes
½ cup blueberries
¼ cup creamed cottage cheese
¼ cup low-fat yogurt
¼ cup white grape juice or apple juice
½ teaspoon curry powder
   dash of ground cinnamon
   dash of ground nutmeg
1 drop lemon extract
   mint sprigs (garnish)

Squeeze the juice from the lemon into a small, shallow bowl. Cut the pineapple into rings, then halve the rings. Peel and slice the kiwi fruits. Halve the nectarines, remove the pits, then slice. Using a melon baller, cut the melon into small balls. Leaving the pears unpeeled, halve them, dipping each piece into the lemon juice.

Place a small bowl in the center of a large, round platter. Beginning at the bowl, curve four rows of nectarine slices out to the edge of the platter in a pinwheel pattern, leaving space between the rows. Next, wash the strawberries and remove the caps. Arrange them in similar rows beside the nectarines. Add the pear halves, placing one beside each row of strawberries, near the bowl. Then add four rows of melon balls. Place the kiwi slices and pineapple pieces near the edge of the platter to fill in the outer edge of the pattern. Add grapes and blueberries to fill in empty spaces.

To prepare the dip, place the cottage cheese, yogurt, grape or apple juice, curry powder, cinnamon, nutmeg and lemon extract in a blender. Process on low to medium speed until smooth, then pour into the bowl at the center of the platter.

Garnish liberally with mint sprigs. If desired, cover the fruit arrangement tightly with plastic wrap and chill before serving.

An impressive array of fruit will set the mood for any festive gathering. Choose fresh, ripe fruits in season for the best effect and most succulent flavor.

Minted Pink Grapefruit Sections ● ●

Makes 4 servings

2 large pink grapefruits
1 tablespoon shredded fresh mint
1 teaspoon sunflower oil
   mint sprigs (garnish)

Peel the grapefruits, removing all of the white membrane. Use a sharp knife to remove the grapefruit sections from the membranes, catching any juice in a small bowl.

In a medium bowl, toss the grapefruit with the mint, oil and the juice from the grapefruit. Place the sections in small bowls set over crushed ice. Garnish with mint sprigs.

Variation: Add fresh orange sections to the grapefruit and garnish with thin strips of orange rind.

Fruit Tray with Stuffed Dates ●

Makes 10 to 16 servings

½ small watermelon
¾ cup Minted Vinaigrette Dressing (page 44)
1 small ripe pineapple, peeled
¼ cup finely minced fresh mint
2 ounces sharp cheddar cheese
10 to 20 pitted dates
   kale leaves (garnish)
   grape clusters (garnish)

Using a melon baller, cut small watermelon balls. Place them in a medium bowl with the dressing, then cover and refrigerate for several hours or overnight.

Quarter the pineapple lengthwise. Remove the tough inner core and cut lengthwise into thin slices. Dust lightly with mint.

Cut the cheese into thin strips and stuff them into the dates. Arrange the stuffed dates on a platter with the melon balls and pineapple. Garnish with kale and grapes.

A Taste of the Middle East

Spinach Triangles ●

A really superior hors d'oeuvre!

Makes 12 servings

1 pound spinach
1 small onion, finely chopped
2 tablespoons virgin olive oil
½ cup chopped scallions
¼ cup minced fresh parsley
2 teaspoons minced fresh dill
   dash of freshly grated nutmeg
½ cup crumbled feta cheese
½ cup creamed cottage cheese
2 eggs, beaten
6 sheets phyllo pastry
⅓ cup Butter-Half (page 133),
   melted

Remove the stems from the spinach and rinse the leaves very well, then chop them. Steam just until wilted. Drain in a colander, pressing out any liquid with a spoon.

Place the onions and oil in a medium skillet. Cook over medium heat until slightly tender. Add the scallions and cook until limp. Remove from heat.

Stir in the parsley, dill, nutmeg, spinach, cheeses and eggs. Set aside.

To make the spinach squares, cut the sheets of phyllo pastry lengthwise into four equal strips. While working with one strip, keep the rest pliable by covering them with a slightly damp, clean cloth.

Brush one strip of phyllo lightly with butter-half. Fold in half lengthwise and brush again with butter-half. Place a spoonful of spinach filling near one end of the strip.

Fold the end of the strip diagonally across the filling, forming a triangle. Fold the triangle straight down to encase the filling, then fold again diagonally across the strip. Continue folding to the end of the strip, forming a fat triangle. Repeat with remaining pastry strips.

Place triangles on a lightly oiled baking sheet and brush lightly with butter-half. Bake in a preheated 350°F oven for 20 minutes, or until puffed and golden. Serve hot.

NOTE: To freeze, place on lightly oiled baking sheets, brush with butter-half and place in the freezer. As soon as the triangles are frozen, carefully remove them from the baking sheets and pack into freezer bags. Seal and store in freezer. Carefully separate triangles when ready to use. Bake as directed for about 25 minutes.

Variation: Substitute 3 tablespoons virgin olive oil and 3 tablespoons melted butter for the butter-half.

Tabbouleh-Stuffed Mushrooms ● ●

An interesting, nutritious, make-ahead hors d'oeuvre.

Makes 12 to 16 servings

⅓ cup bulgur
⅓ cup water
3 tablespoons lemon juice
20 to 24 very large mushrooms
½ cup finely chopped tomatoes
⅓ cup minced fresh parsley
⅓ cup minced fresh spinach
¼ cup minced scallions
1 tablespoon minced fresh mint
3 tablespoons sunflower oil
   cherry tomatoes (garnish)
   large mint sprigs (garnish)

Place the bulgur, water and lemon juice in a large bowl. Allow the bulgur to soak for 20 to 30 minutes, or until it is soft and all of the liquid has been absorbed.

Remove the stems from the mushrooms. (Save them for another purpose, such as adding to soups or omelets.)

Place the mushroom caps in a large saucepan half filled with boiling water. Return the water to a boil, then reduce heat, cover and simmer 3 to 4 minutes, until the mushrooms are firm-tender. Drain and allow to cool.

To make the tabbouleh, add the tomatoes, parsley, spinach, scallions, mint and oil to the softened bulgur. Toss until well combined.

Spoon the tabbouleh into the mushroom caps. If desired, cover with foil and refrigerate before serving. Garnish the serving plate lavishly with cherry tomatoes and mint.

Hummus Tahini ●●

Use this as a party dip for raw vegetables, whole grain crackers or the traditional pita bread.

Makes 3½ cups

 2 tablespoons chopped parsley
 2 garlic cloves, minced
 ½ cup sesame tahini
 ½ cup lemon juice
 ½ cup olive oil
 ½ cup water
 2 cups cooked chick-peas
    dash of cayenne pepper
    parsley sprigs (garnish)

Place the chopped parsley, garlic, tahini, lemon juice, oil and water in a blender. Process on low speed until smooth.

Add half the chick-peas and process on low speed until smooth. Add the remaining chick-peas and continue to process until smooth, stopping to scrape down the sides as necessary.

Place the tahini in one or more serving bowls. Sprinkle with a dash of cayenne and garnish with parsley. Refrigerate leftovers, tightly covered.

Camembert Torte
● ●

An aristocratic hors d'oeuvre for parties and large get-togethers. Place a fancy doilie under the cheese and garnish with parsley sprigs, mint or even fresh flowers.

Accompanied by fresh fruit, Camembert Torte is an elegant, Continental-style dessert.

Makes 30 to 45 servings

1 12-inch wheel Camembert cheese
   (about 3½ pounds)
1 pound cream cheese
½ cup sweet butter
1 cup sliced almonds
   parsley or mint sprigs (garnish)

Cut the wheel of Camembert into two layers. Remove the top layer and set aside.

Place the cream cheese and butter in a medium bowl. Using a wooden spoon, cream them together until soft.

Spread about one-third of the cream cheese mixture on the bottom layer of the Camembert. Sprinkle with some of the almonds.

Replace the top layer and spread the top and sides of the torte with the remaining cream cheese mixture. Sprinkle with almonds.

Place parsley or mint around the perimeter of the serving plate. Using a very sharp knife, cut the torte into very thin wedges and serve, accompanied by rye and whole wheat crackers.

Herbed Cheese Spread ● ●

Pass up the expensive French *boursin* by making your own tasty facsimile.

Makes about ¾ cup

⅓ cup farmer's cheese
3 tablespoons cream cheese
¼ cup finely minced fresh chives
3 tablespoons finely minced fresh parsley
1 tablespoon freshly grated Parmesan cheese
½ to 1 garlic clove
¼ teaspoon dried marjoram
¼ teaspoon dried basil
 freshly ground black pepper
 finely minced fresh parsley (garnish)

Place the farmer's cheese and cream cheese in a shallow bowl. Using a wooden spoon, cream them together.

Add the chives, parsley and Parmesan cheese, the garlic, pushed through a garlic press, and the herbs, crumbled between your fingers. Add some pepper to taste.

Blend the cheese and herb mixture until combined. Either pack the herbed cheese into a small crock or form into a flattened round. Dust with parsley. Chill, if desired.

Chevre Spread ● ●

Tangy chevre, a goat cheese, gets a touch of herb and spice for a unique hors d'oeuvre.

Makes 1 cup

1 cup crumbled chevre cheese
¼ cup olive oil
½ teaspoon crumbled dried rosemary
 dash of ground cloves

Combine the cheese with the oil, rosemary and a light dusting of cloves.

Pack the spread into a small crock and serve with crackers or raw vegetables. If chilled, allow the spread to return to room temperature before serving.

NOTE: Chevre cheese is expensive and can be difficult to find. You can substitute feta, also a goat cheese, but the flavor will be somewhat different.

Roquefort Spread ●

Makes ¾ cup

⅓ cup Roquefort cheese, crumbled
2 tablespoons cream cheese
¼ cup cottage cheese
⅛ teaspoon caraway seeds

Place the Roquefort and cream cheese in a small bowl and cream them together with the back of a spoon.

Stir in the cottage cheese and caraway seeds.

Pack the spread into a small crock or serving bowl. Chill, tightly covered, until ready to serve. Accompany the spread with whole grain crackers or raw vegetables.

Nachos Platter ● ●

Makes 4 servings

2 cups Chili con Carne (page 87)
  Tortilla Chips (this page)
¾ cup shredded sharp cheddar cheese
½ cup Guacamole Dip (opposite
    page)

Heat the chili. Arrange half the
tortilla chips in a shallow 9 × 13-
inch baking dish and spoon the
chili over them.

Arrange the remaining chips
over the chili. Sprinkle with cheese.
Bake in a preheated 350°F oven for
about 15 minutes, or until the cheese
has melted.

Top the hot nachos with dollops
of guacamole dip, or serve the dip on
the side.

NOTE: Served with a large salad, the
nachos platter makes a good main
dish for two.

Tortilla Chips ● ●

Makes 4 servings

8 corn tortillas, quartered
¼ cup safflower oil

Place the oil in a small, heavy-
bottom skillet. Heat until a slightly
wavy pattern appears on the surface
of the oil.

Cook four sections of tortilla at a
time, removing them when they are
crisp and golden. Drain on paper
towels.

**Crisp tortilla chips, spicy chili
and tangy guacamole dip combine to make this Nachos Platter a favorite at any get-together.**

Mexican Bean Dip
● ●

Makes 1½ cups

```
1 cup cooked red kidney beans
½ cup yogurt
½ small onion, coarsely chopped
1 garlic clove, minced
1 tablespoon Homemade Chili
    Seasoning (page 87)
  chopped scallions (garnish)
```

Place the beans, yogurt, onions, garlic and chili seasoning in a blender. Process on medium speed until smooth. Pour into a small bowl and garnish with chopped scallions.

Serve with cauliflower and broccoli florets, zucchini sticks, cucumber slices, celery sticks and Jerusalem artichoke slices, along with other favorite raw vegetables, arranged on a large platter around the dip.

Guacamole Dip ● ●

Makes 6 servings

```
2 medium ripe avocados
¼ cup lemon juice
2 garlic cloves
¼ cup chopped sweet Spanish onion
½ cup sour cream or Whole Egg
    Mayonnaise (page 48)
```

Peel the avocados, remove the pits and chop coarsely.

Place the avocado in a blender or food processor with the lemon juice, the garlic, pushed through a garlic press, the onion and sour cream or mayonnaise. Process on low to medium speed until smooth, stopping to scrape down the sides as necessary.

The Well-Kept Avocado

If you are planning to use only half of an avocado, cut it lengthwise. Tightly wrap the remaining half, *with the pit*, and store it in the refrigerator. The pit will help keep the remaining portion of avocado from darkening. Made-ahead avocado dips also can be kept bright by pushing the pit into the center of the dish. Cover and chill. Remove the pit and stir the dip before serving. Lemon juice will also preserve the fresh green color of avocados.

Spoon the blended mixture into a serving dish. If desired, chill, tightly covered, before serving. (Stir before serving if the top of the dip discolors slightly.) Serve with Tortilla Chips (opposite page) or raw vegetables.

NOTE: For guacamole with more body, reserve half of the avocado. Mash it with a fork, then add it to the blended mixture.

A Make-Ahead Party for 25

Put together a party and forget about dinner. If you serve an assortment of nutritious hors d'oeuvres, your guests can select what they want and eat as much as they wish.

The Day before the Party. Prepare the Baba Ghannouj. Fill the Cheese-Topped Mushroom Caps with Spinach. Refrigerate them until it's time to heat them for the party.

The Day of the Party. Cut the raw vegetables for Crudites with Sour Cream Dip. Moisten them and place in a plastic bag in the refrigerator. Prepare the dip, cover and refrigerate.

At the Last Minute. Make the sauce for the Pesto-Stuffed Eggs and stuff the eggs at the last minute so that they do not discolor.

When the eggplant is cool enough to handle, peel off the charred skin and discard it. Place the pulp in a blender or food processor and process on medium speed until smooth. Stir it into the tahini mixture. Serve at room temperature, garnished with parsley.

NOTE: To give the dip more texture, finely chop all or part of the eggplant with a knife before stirring it into the tahini mixture, instead of pureeing it.

Baba Ghannouj ●●

A typical dip of the Middle East, based on eggplant and garlic.

Makes 2 cups

1 medium eggplant
2 garlic cloves
⅓ cup sesame tahini
3 tablespoons lemon juice
½ teaspoon tamari
   dash of cayenne pepper
1 tablespoon minced fresh parsley
   (garnish)

Pierce the eggplant with a fork in several spots. Place the whole eggplant in a broiler about 4 inches from the heating element. Turning it occasionally, cook the eggplant until it is soft and begins to collapse. The skin will be charred.

Set the eggplant aside to cool. In a medium bowl, combine the garlic, pushed through a garlic press, the tahini, lemon juice, tamari and cayenne.

Stuffed Tiny Red Potatoes ●●●

Serve as an appetizer or as part of a buffet.

Makes 12 to 24 servings

24 tiny new red potatoes
¾ cup Sour Yogurt-Cream (page 132)
2 tablespoons minced fresh chives
   paprika (garnish)
2 to 3 bunches watercress
   (garnish)

Steam the potatoes (they should be about "two-bite" size) until they are readily pierced with a fork, 8 to 10 minutes.

On a flat surface, test the potatoes to see how they will best lie flat. Then use a knife to partially hollow out the top of each potato.

Place a dollop of sour yogurt-cream in each hollowed-out potato. Top with chives and dust with paprika.

Arrange the watercress on serving plates, then add the potatoes.

NOTE: Do not chill the potatoes before filling. If desired, the potatoes can be hollowed out and held, covered, at room temperature, until serving time. Add sour yogurt-cream just before serving.

Crudites with Sour Cream Dip ● ●

This dip is so economical that even the scallion roots go to good use, giving a tangy onion flavor to the dip.

Makes 12 servings

½ cup sour cream
¼ cup yogurt
1 tablespoon minced fresh parsley
½ to 1 teaspoon minced scallion
    roots
¼ teaspoon dried marjoram
¼ teaspoon dried oregano
    dash of cayenne pepper
1 zucchini
1 yellow squash
1 stalk celery
2 carrots
12 scallions

To make the dip, combine the sour cream, yogurt, parsley and scallion roots in a small bowl. (Before mincing, rinse the roots thoroughly under running water. Discard the thin segment where the roots are attached to the scallion.)

Add the herbs and cayenne. Stir well and chill until ready to serve.

Cut the zucchini, squash, celery and carrots into long, thin strips or rounds. Arrange, along with the scallions, around the bowl of dip.

Pesto-Stuffed Eggs ● ●

An easy, exciting hors d'oeuvre!

Makes 6 to 12 servings

6 eggs
⅓ cup Pesto Sauce (page 108)
1 tablespoon safflower oil
    fresh basil leaves (garnish)

To hard-cook the eggs, prick the large ends with a push pin so they do not crack during cooking. Fill a large saucepan three-fourths full of water and bring to a boil. Lower the eggs into the water with a ladle.

Return the water to a boil, then reduce heat and simmer 12 minutes. Drain and place the eggs under cold running water to stop further cooking.

Remove the shells and halve the eggs lengthwise. Reserve the yolks from seven of the egg halves for another use. Place the remaining yolks in a mixing bowl with the pesto sauce and oil. Stir until thoroughly combined.

Spoon the pesto filling back into the egg halves, or use a pastry bag with a star tip to pipe the filling into the eggs. Garnish with fresh basil leaves.

Cheese-Topped Mushroom Caps with Spinach ● ●

Makes 8 servings

8 very large mushrooms
2 tablespoons butter
1 small onion, minced
¼ cup grated carrots
1 cup packed spinach leaves
2 tablespoons sunflower seeds
1 tablespoon minced fresh parsley
1 teaspoon tamari
2 tablespoons shredded Gruyere
    or Swiss cheese

Carefully remove the stems from the mushroom caps. Melt the butter in a medium skillet. Add the mushroom caps and stems and cook until they give up their liquid and it has evaporated.

Remove the mushrooms and set aside. Place the onions and carrots in the skillet. Cook until the onions are translucent and begin to get tender.

Chop the spinach and the mushroom stems. Add them to the skillet and cook, stirring constantly, until the spinach is wilted and any excess water has evaporated. Turn off heat.

Place the sunflower seeds in a blender. Process with short bursts at high speed until ground. Stir into the spinach mixture, along with the parsley and tamari.

Stuff the mushroom caps with the spinach mixture. Top with cheese. Cover and refrigerate until ready to serve.

Place the stuffed mushrooms in a shallow baking dish in a preheated 350°F oven for 15 minutes. Serve hot.

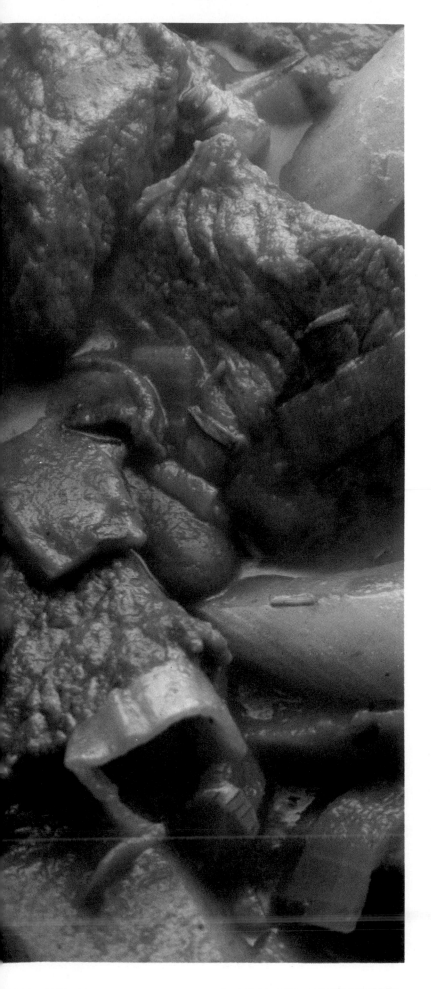

Make the Most of Meat

Too much of a good thing, that's the trouble with meat. But used wisely, it's still a star.

S teak 'n' potatoes have long been considered the makings of a fine meal—with the emphasis always on the steak. Red meats, however, can be high in calories and in saturated fats, two of several reasons why people moving toward a healthier diet begin by cutting down on meats.

However, red meats should not be dismissed too quickly. High in potassium, B vitamins, zinc and iron, they can add much toward making a diet healthy. Perhaps the role meat plays in our menu should be reevaluated. Instead of being the star—center-stage at every meal—maybe meats can be put to best use in a supporting role. To that end, the recipes in this section are designed to take best advantage of meat's strong points and provide a counterpoint to its weaknesses. While you won't find recipes for he-man roasts or slabs of ham, you will find an unusual variety of dishes that, nevertheless, will satisfy your hunger for meat.

For one thing, you'll notice that they combine meat with vegetables, rice or beans—ingredients that provide the fiber that meat lacks. Fiber, as you know, helps in fighting heart disease, digestive disorders and certain types of cancer. In addition to these preventive health aspects, adding fiber to meat dishes also helps us feel satisfied sooner, thus providing a natural way to reduce our intake of calorie-rich meats.

To further limit calories and saturated fats, always buy the leanest cuts, then trim off any visible fat before cooking. If you saute ground meat, drain away any fat released by cooking before adding the meat to sauces and other dishes.

You still can enjoy meat and reap its health benefits by preparing these tasty recipes that use this ingredient in moderation.

Stuffed Red Peppers
●

Makes 4 servings

  4 large sweet red peppers
  1 tablespoon corn oil
  1 medium onion, chopped
  ½ pound lean ground beef
  ¼ cup finely chopped walnuts
  2 garlic cloves, minced
1½ cups cooked brown rice
  ½ cup diced cooked potatoes
  1 tablespoon tamari
  1 teaspoon dried marjoram
  ¼ teaspoon ground coriander
1½ to 2 cups Tomato Sauce (page 116)
  parsley sprigs (garnish)

Halve the peppers lengthwise, or cut off the tops, and remove the seeds. Steam for just a few minutes, until they begin to soften. Set aside.

Place the oil and onions in a large skillet and cook until translucent. Add the beef and brown it. Add a few drops of water, if needed, to prevent sticking.

Stuffed Red Peppers look zingy and taste zesty—just the thing to pep up a tired menu.

Add the walnuts, garlic, rice, potatoes, tamari, marjoram and coriander. Heat through.

Lightly oil a shallow 9 × 13-inch baking dish. Pour in enough tomato sauce to just cover the bottom of the dish.

Fill the peppers with the meat mixture and arrange them in the baking dish. If desired, spoon some tomato sauce over the stuffed peppers.

Bake, uncovered, in a preheated 350°F oven for 30 minutes.

Variations: Use 2 cups of rice and omit the potatoes, or use 1 cup of rice and 1 cup of potatoes.

Arrange thin slices of mozzarella cheese over the peppers.

Stuffed Vine Leaves
● ●

Makes 4 to 6 servings

  1 large onion, chopped
  3 tablespoons olive oil
  1 cup uncooked brown rice
1¾ cups Low-Sodium Chicken Stock (page 52)
  1 tablespoon tamari
  1 tablespoon lemon juice
40 to 50 grape leaves
  ¼ pound lean ground beef or lamb
  ¼ cup pine nuts
  ¼ cup currants or chopped raisins
  2 tablespoons minced fresh dill
  2 teaspoons minced fresh mint
  ½ teaspoon ground cinnamon
  ¼ teaspoon ground allspice
  3 lemons
  2 cups water
  yogurt (garnish)
  mint sprigs (garnish)

Place the onions with the oil in a large saucepan. Cook over medium heat until translucent.

Stir in the rice, and when it has absorbed the oil, add the stock, tamari and lemon juice.

Bring the rice to a boil. Stir, then reduce heat to lowest setting, cover tightly and steam the rice for 40 minutes. Remove from heat and keep covered until ready to use.

Bring a large pot of water to a boil. Place the grape leaves, a few at a

Stuffed Vine Leaves, traditional Middle Eastern fare, can be served as a main dish or as an exotic appetizer.

time, in the boiling water for about 3 minutes. Rinse each batch under cold running water and set aside.

Brown the beef or lamb in a small skillet. Drain off fat.

In a large bowl, combine the rice, beef or lamb, pine nuts, currants or raisins, dill, mint, cinnamon and allspice.

To stuff the vine leaves, place large, whole leaves shiny-side down on a cutting board. Use a sharp knife to remove the stems and tough center ribs.

Place about 1 tablespoon of filling on each large vine leaf at the stem end. Roll up slightly, just to enclose the filling, then fold in the sides of the leaf. Continue rolling until the vine leaf is a neat package.

Cover the bottom of a large ovenproof casserole with small or torn leaves. Add one layer of stuffed leaves.

Cut one of the lemons into thin slices. Place 3 or 4 slices on top of the first layer of stuffed vine leaves. Add remaining stuffed leaves in layers and cover with a few slices of lemon.

When all of the stuffed vine leaves are placed in the casserole, top them with enough small or torn leaves to cover completely. Pour the water over the leaves. Place an ovenproof plate on top of the vine leaves to weigh them down.

Bake in a preheated 350°F oven for 1 to 1¼ hours, or until the leaves are tender.

Serve the vine leaves at room temperature or chilled. Arrange on the serving plate and top with dollops of yogurt, or serve yogurt separately. Garnish with the remaining lemons, cut into wedges, and mint sprigs.

NOTE: Stuffed vine leaves can be used as an hors d'oeuvre, serving 10 to 12 people. Provide a bowl of yogurt for dipping.

Sweet-and-Sour Beef Stew ●

A delicious, if surprising, approach to stew. The surprise? Pears!

Makes 6 servings

¼ cup water
3 tablespoons cider vinegar
2 tablespoons light unsulfured molasses
1 tablespoon tamari
1 pound lean beef cubes
3 tablespoons whole wheat flour
1 tablespoon safflower oil
5 cups Vegetable Stock (page 53) or Low-Sodium Chicken Stock (page 52)
1 medium onion, chopped
4 carrots
3 stalks celery
12 small white onions
½ cup tomato paste
2 large very firm pears
¼ cup minced fresh parsley

Combine the water, vinegar, molasses and tamari in a medium bowl. Stir until smooth. Cut the beef cubes into small bite-size pieces, then add to the marinade, cover and refrigerate several hours or overnight.

Drain thoroughly, reserving the marinade. Pat the meat dry, then dredge in flour.

In a large, heavy-bottom saucepan or pot, heat the oil. Add the meat and brown it over medium-high heat. Do not try to brown more than a single layer of meat at a time; remove the beef cubes from the pan as they brown.

Return all the beef cubes to the pan and add the marinade, stock and onions. Set over medium heat and bring to a boil, then reduce heat to simmer.

Meanwhile, cut the carrots into 2-inch lengths. Cut the thickest part of the carrots in half lengthwise. Cut the celery into 2-inch lengths, again cutting the thickest section in half lengthwise. Peel the small onions, but leave them whole.

Add the vegetables and tomato paste to the pan. Return to a boil, then cover, reduce heat and simmer 1 hour and 15 minutes, stirring occasionally.

Cut the pears into large cubes. Add them to the stew and cook an additional 20 to 30 minutes, until the pears are tender but not mushy.

Add the parsley just before removing the stew from the heat. Serve hot over brown rice.

Baked Meatloaf with Pimiento Topping

Makes 8 servings

¾ cup cooked chick-peas
¼ cup raw sunflower seeds
1 carrot, shredded
4 scallions, chopped
2 eggs, beaten
1 pound lean ground beef
½ cup soft whole wheat bread crumbs
3 tablespoons tomato paste
1 tablespoon tamari
8 strips pimiento
3 tablespoons water
parsley sprigs (garnish)

In a blender, food processor or food mill, grind the chick-peas into meal. (In the blender use short bursts at high speed; in the processor, use the steel blade.) Repeat with the sunflower seeds.

Mix together the chick-pea and sunflower seed meal with the carrots, scallions, eggs, beef, 2 tablespoons of tomato paste and tamari. Pack into a 9 × 5-inch loaf pan.

Decorate the top of the meatloaf with strips of pimiento. In a small bowl, mix together 1 tablespoon of tomato paste and the water. Spoon over top of the meatloaf.

Cover the pan loosely with foil. Bake in a preheated 350°F oven for 1 hour, removing the foil after 30 minutes. Garnish with parsley.

NOTE: To prepare pimiento, place a sweet red pepper under a broiler until the skin is bubbled and charred and the pepper is soft. Wrap in a damp towel for 10 minutes, remove charred skin and cut pepper into strips.

Beef and Vegetable Stew ●●

Makes 10 servings

¼ cup dried Oriental mushrooms
10 cups water
¼ cup corn oil
1 pound lean beef cubes
1 large onion, chopped
1 sweet Spanish onion, chopped
2 large leeks, chopped
1 cup chopped celery
8 carrots, sliced diagonally
1 cup fresh mushrooms
2 cups tomato puree
6 to 8 garlic cloves, minced
2 bay leaves
1 teaspoon dried basil
½ teaspoon dried marjoram
¼ teaspoon dried thyme
¼ teaspoon dried oregano
¼ teaspoon dried tarragon
⅛ teaspoon ground allspice
2 cups cooked kidney beans
6 cups cubed potatoes
⅔ cup tomato paste
2 tablespoons chopped fresh chives
    or minced fresh parsley
3 tablespoons tamari

Soak the dried mushrooms for about 1 hour in 1 cup of the water. Drain the mushrooms and reserve the soaking liquid. Chop the mushrooms.

Place the oil in a large kettle or stockpot. Add the beef cubes, in one layer, and saute until browned on all sides.

Add the remaining water, the onions, leeks, celery, carrots, fresh mushrooms, tomato puree, garlic, bay leaves, herbs and allspice.

Bring to a boil and skim off any foam that rises to the surface. Reduce heat, cover and simmer for 2 hours, stirring occasionally.

Add the kidney beans, potatoes and tomato paste. Simmer the stew an additional 30 minutes. Stir in the chives or parsley and tamari and remove the bay leaves. Serve hot.

Cider-Braised Lamb with Apricots ●●

Makes 10 servings

2 tablespoons corn oil
1 large onion, chopped
2 tablespoons butter
2 pounds lamb cubes
¾ cup dried apricot halves
½ cup raisins
¼ cup chopped pitted prunes
1 teaspoon ground cinnamon
3 cups apple cider
2 cups Low-Sodium Chicken Stock
    (page 52)
2 cups uncooked brown rice
3½ cups water

In a large skillet, use 1 tablespoon of the corn oil to saute the onions until lightly browned. Add a few drops of water, if necessary, to prevent sticking. Remove the onions and set aside.

Add the remaining oil and 1 tablespoon of the butter. When the butter has melted, add about half the lamb and cook until the cubes have browned on all sides. Remove them from the pan, scraping out any bits of meat.

Add the remaining butter and the remaining lamb cubes and brown them.

Place the onions, lamb, apricots, raisins, prunes, cinnamon, cider and stock in a large stockpot or kettle. Bring to a boil, then reduce heat, cover and simmer for 2 hours, stirring occasionally.

When the lamb has simmered about 1½ hours, combine the rice and water in a medium saucepan. Bring to a boil, then cover and reduce heat as low as possible. Simmer for 30 minutes, then remove from heat.

In a very large, ovenproof casserole, alternate layers of rice and lamb, beginning with half the rice mixture. Bake, uncovered, in a preheated 350°F oven for 45 minutes. Serve hot.

Le Chef's

Natural Meat Tenderizers

Use the following ingredients and techniques to soften a tough cut of meat.

Lemon juice
Vinegar
Stewing
Grinding
Pounding
Marinating
Braising

Spicy Meat Turnovers ● ●

Appetizing for dinner or buffet and suitable for picnic fare, too!

Makes 12 servings

Pastry
  1 tablespoon active dry yeast
  ¼ cup lukewarm water
  1 cup lukewarm buttermilk
  2 tablespoons safflower oil
3¼ to 3½ cups whole wheat flour
  1 egg
  1 egg white
  1 teaspoon honey
Filling
  1 large onion, chopped
  2 tablespoons safflower oil
  ½ pound lean ground beef
  2 tablespoons tomato paste
  4 teaspoons Homemade Chili Sea-
      soning (page 87) or chili
      powder
  1 teaspoon ground cumin
  ½ cup raisins
  ½ cup water
Glaze
  1 egg yolk
  1 tablespoon water

In a large bowl, dissolve the yeast in the lukewarm water. When the yeast mixture is foamy, add the buttermilk, oil and 1¾ cups of flour.

Beat the mixture for about 3 minutes with an electric mixer on low speed. Cover the bowl with a cloth and allow the dough to rise for 30 minutes.

Stir it down and add 1 cup of flour, the egg, egg white and honey. Beat them together with a wooden spoon.

Add enough flour to make a soft dough, then knead it on a floured surface until soft and elastic. Oil the bowl, return the dough to the bowl and turn it to oil all sides. Cover and let rise until doubled in bulk, about 1 hour.

Punch down the dough, then cover the bowl and set aside.

To prepare the filling, place the onions in a large skillet with the oil. Cook, stirring occasionally, over medium heat until lightly browned.

Add the meat and stir until cooked through. Add the tomato paste, chili seasoning, cumin, raisins and water and cook an additional 5 minutes, stirring frequently. Remove from heat.

Punch down the dough and divide it in half. Divide each half into six pieces and then divide each of these in half, making a total of 24 small balls of dough.

Flatten each ball of dough by hand, then place it on an oiled plate and stretch it out into a circle 4 inches across. (You can also roll out the dough into circles on a floured surface.)

Place a rounded tablespoon of filling in the center of the dough. Pull one side of the dough up and around the filling to meet the opposite edge, making a half circle. Use the tines of a fork to seal the edges. Repeat with remaining dough.

Place the turnovers on two baking sheets. Combine the egg yolk and water and brush the turnovers with the glaze. Let rise 10 to 15 minutes, then bake in a preheated 400°F oven for 25 minutes, or until golden brown and puffed.

Oriental Cabbage Rolls ● ●

Makes 8 servings

Pastry
  1 tablespoon active dry yeast
  ¼ cup lukewarm water
  1 cup lukewarm buttermilk
  2 tablespoons safflower oil
3¼ to 3½ cups whole wheat flour
  1 egg
  1 egg white
Filling
  ½ pound lean ground beef
  3 cups finely shredded cabbage
  1 cup mung bean sprouts
  1 tablespoon tamari
1½ teaspoons ground peeled
      ginger root
  3 garlic cloves, minced
Glaze
  1 egg yolk
  1 tablespoon water

Dip
    2 tablespoons tamari
    1 tablespoon vinegar
    1 teaspoon water
    ¼ teaspoon sesame oil

In a small bowl, dissolve the yeast in the lukewarm water. When the yeast mixture is foamy, place it in a large bowl with the buttermilk. Add the oil and 1¾ cups of flour.

Beat the mixture for about 3 minutes with an electric mixer on low to medium speed. Cover the bowl with a cloth and set aside to rise for about 30 minutes.

Stir down the mixture and add 1 cup of flour, the egg and egg white. Beat them together with a wooden spoon.

Add enough flour to make a soft dough, then knead it on a floured surface until it is soft and elastic. Oil the bowl, return the dough to the bowl and turn it to oil all sides. Cover and let rise until doubled in bulk, 45 to 60 minutes.

Punch down the dough, then cover the bowl and set aside.

To prepare the filling, brown the meat in a small skillet. Then drain and crumble the meat.

In a medium bowl, combine the cabbage with the bean sprouts, the meat, tamari, ginger and garlic.

Punch down the dough and divide it in half. Divide each half into six pieces, then divide each piece in half, making a total of 24 small balls of dough.

Roll out the dough into circles 4 inches across. Place some of the filling in each circle. To enclose it, pull both sides of the dough over the filling. Pinch to seal. Pull the remaining two sides toward the center and pinch. Continue around the circumference of the circle. Repeat with remaining dough.

Place the rolls seam-side down on lightly oiled baking sheets. Combine the egg yolk and water and brush the rolls with the glaze. Let rise for 10 to 15 minutes, then bake in a preheated 350°F oven for 20 to 25 minutes, until the rolls are golden.

While the rolls are baking, make the dip by combining the tamari, vinegar, water and oil.

Serve the rolls with dip, spooned into tiny bowls at each place setting.

Variation: For a vegetarian main dish, substitute uncooked crumbled tofu for the ground beef.

Leek and Walnut Meatloaf

Walnuts add texture to this flavorful main dish.

Makes 8 servings

    3 large leeks, chopped
    2 tablespoons sunflower oil
    1½ cups cubed potatoes
    ⅓ cup chopped walnuts
    ¾ pound lean ground beef
    2 eggs
    1 cup whole wheat bread crumbs
    2 tablespoons tamari
    ⅛ teaspoon dried marjoram
    ⅛ teaspoon dried thyme
    2 tablespoons tomato paste
    2 tablespoons apple cider

In a large skillet, cook the leeks in the oil over medium heat until tender but not browned. Place the potatoes in a large pot of water. Bring to a boil, then reduce heat, partially cover and simmer until the potatoes are tender. Drain and lightly mash the potatoes.

In a small skillet, lightly toast the walnuts over low to medium heat, stirring often. Place them in a large bowl with the leeks, potatoes, beef, eggs, bread crumbs, tamari and herbs. Stir to combine.

Pack this mixture into a 9 × 5-inch loaf pan. Mix the tomato paste and cider and spoon over the meatloaf. Bake 1 hour in a preheated 350°F oven. Remove from oven and let stand about 10 minutes before serving.

Mexican Cooking

Beef and Lentil Tacos ● ●

These tacos are very tasty, and the lentils add a bonus of fiber.

Makes 6 servings

1 onion, chopped
1 tablespoon sunflower oil
2 garlic cloves, minced
1 pound lean ground beef
1 cup cooked lentils
¼ cup water
2 tablespoons Homemade Chili
    Seasoning (opposite page)
2 tablespoons tomato paste
12 taco shells
1 cup Hot Chili Sauce (this page)
2 tomatoes, seeded and chopped
1 small onion, chopped (optional)
2 cups chopped lettuce
½ cup alfalfa sprouts

In a large skillet, cook the onions in the oil until tender.

Stir in the garlic and add the beef. Break the meat apart as it cooks.

When the meat is browned, add the lentils, water, chili seasoning and tomato paste. Stir well to combine.

Simmer the meat mixture over low heat. Warm the taco shells in a preheated 350°F oven.

To assemble the tacos, place some of the filling in each taco shell. Add a dash of chili sauce.

Top with chopped tomatoes, onion, if desired, lettuce and sprouts. Serve hot.

Hot Chili Sauce

Give a fiery lift—Mexican style—to tacos, tortillas, enchiladas or eggs. When you make your own hot chili sauce, you'll have a spicy seasoning that's rich in fiber and vitamin C.

Use 1 or 2 fresh hot chili peppers, according to your taste. Cut the peppers open and discard the seeds and inner membranes. To make about 3 cups of the hot sauce, place 3 tablespoons of safflower or sunflower oil in a medium heavy-bottom skillet. Add 1 large onion, finely chopped, and 1 or 2 fresh hot chili peppers.

Cook the onions and peppers over medium heat, stirring frequently, for about 5 minutes.

Add to the skillet 2 cups of peeled and finely chopped tomatoes with their juice. Bring to a boil. Reduce heat, cover and simmer about 10 minutes, stirring occasionally.

Freeze the sauce in a tightly covered container, or simply refrigerate, if it will be used promptly.

Chili con Carne ● ●

Makes 10 to 12 servings

2 cups chopped celery
1 cup chopped onions
¼ cup safflower oil
1 cup finely grated carrots
1 pound lean ground beef
4 cups cooked red kidney beans
8 cups tomatoes, peeled and crushed
    or chopped (with juice)
4 garlic cloves
2 tablespoons Homemade Chili
    Seasoning (this page)
½ teaspoon dried oregano
2 tablespoons tamari

In a large, heavy-bottom saucepan place the celery and onions with 3 tablespoons of the oil. Cook until translucent.

Stir in the carrots. Stir and cook until the vegetables begin to soften. Remove vegetables from the pan and set aside.

Add the remaining tablespoon of oil to the pan. Saute the beef until it is browned. Drain the fat.

Stir in the vegetables, beans and tomatoes. Add the garlic, pushed through a garlic press or minced, and the chili seasoning and oregano.

Bring to a boil, then reduce heat and simmer for 25 to 30 minutes. Stir in the tamari and serve, accompanied by whole grain rolls and a salad.

Variations: Chili con carne can be served in taco shells, on tostadas or wrapped in tortillas, for enchiladas.

Mexican Meatballs ●

Makes 6 servings

1 pound lean ground beef
½ cup stone-ground cornmeal
1 egg, beaten
1 tablespoon tomato paste
1 tablespoon minced fresh parsley
½ teaspoon dried oregano
2 teaspoons safflower oil
6 tomatoes, chopped
2 garlic cloves
3 tablespoons tomato paste
1 tablespoon Homemade Chili
    Seasoning (this page) or chili
    powder
1 tablespoon tamari
1 cup water
1½ cups corn kernels
1 cup chopped spinach leaves

In a medium bowl, combine the beef, cornmeal, egg, tomato paste, parsley and oregano. Form into 24 small meatballs.

In a large skillet, warm the oil, then add the meatballs and brown over medium heat. When the meatballs have browned on all sides, add the tomatoes, the garlic, pushed through a garlic press, the tomato paste, chili, tamari and water.

Bring to a boil, then reduce heat, cover and simmer 20 minutes, stirring occasionally.

Add the corn and simmer an additional 10 minutes. Add the spinach and stir just until the spinach is wilted. Serve hot.

Homemade Chili Seasoning

Forgo commercial chili powder, which often has added salt. Instead, make your own flavorful blend to give special character to your Mexican meals. Combine 3 tablespoons pure, ground chili pepper with 1½ tablespoons ground cumin, 1 teaspoon dried oregano, ½ teaspoon cayenne pepper, ½ teaspoon dried (rubbed) sage and ½ teaspoon ground allspice.

Store this mixture in a cool, dry place, in a tightly covered small jar.

8

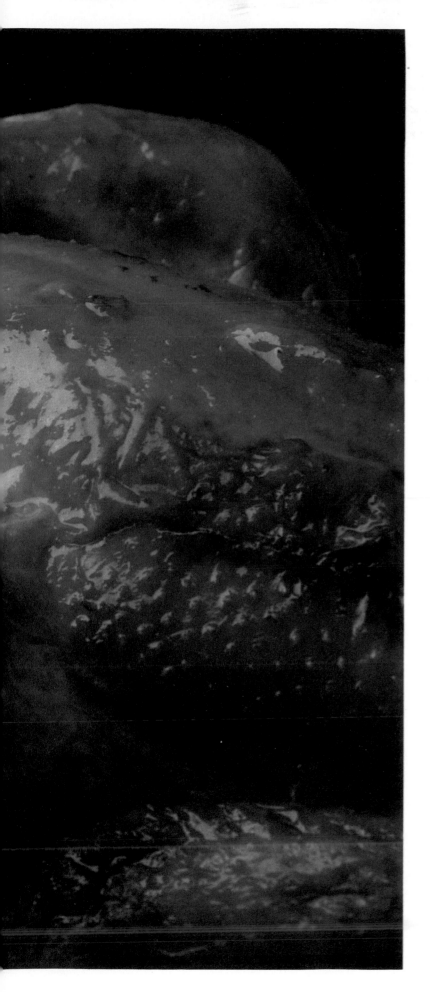

Poultry: Delicate, Adaptable

High in protein, low in fat—poultry is featured in the cuisines of every land.

Poultry is special. Like other meats, it has lots of protein and B vitamins, but it also has fewer calories per serving than either beef or pork. To top it all off, poultry is versatile. Its gentle, rather discreet flavor lends itself to any number of cooking variations. Flavors range from delicate to incendiary, depending on the way the poultry is cooked. It never has to be boring.

For example, we've cooked up some wonderful ways with chicken, each one different and delicious. They range from the elegant, company-for-dinner Dijon Chicken in Phyllo to Enchiladas con Pollo, a casual dish with a South-of-the-Border accent. Serve it with Guacamole Dip and raw vegetables to carry out the Mexican theme. These two recipes keep chicken under wraps. But one of our favorite ways with chicken is stuffed.

Traditionally, you stuff a whole bird, as we do with the recipe for Roasted Game Hens. But for a surprising alternative, try Chicken Legs Stuffed with Herbed Mushrooms. The dark, tender and moist chicken meat is a tasty choice, complemented with a rich, woodsy filling.

Slow-Baked Ginger Chicken and Peggy's Chinese Chicken Salad lean toward the Oriental. And speaking of salad, we've offered two additional salads that bring out the cool best of chicken. Minted Chicken Salad is an herbed best bet for summer fare!

If you want to save money preparing these recipes, purchase whole chickens. That way you will have chicken breasts, thighs and legs for use in a variety of recipes. And you'll also have the necks, backs and bones for making your own rich stock. (See chapter 5.)

If you're headed for healthier meals, make chicken a part of your game plan.

Lower the Fat Level in Poultry

To cut down on calories and saturated fat, prepare skinless chicken breasts by poaching or baking them. In contrast, an equal serving of unskinned chicken that has been batter-dipped and fried contains more than 5 times the total amount of fat, including 4 times more saturated fat. With careful preparation, you can save 135 calories per half-breast serving.

Grilled Chicken with Peanut Sauce ●

Makes 4 servings

2 chicken breasts, boned and skinned
2 teaspoons corn oil
½ cup water
¼ cup peanut butter
1 tablespoon tamari
2 teaspoons light unsulfured molasses
½ teaspoon minced hot pepper
1 garlic clove, minced
1 teaspoon lemon juice
1 tablespoon chopped peanuts (garnish)

Cut the chicken into bite-size pieces. Dry them thoroughly, then coat lightly with the oil. Place the chicken pieces on eight skewers and place under a broiler just until cooked through, turning several times.

While the chicken is cooking, make the sauce. Bring the water to a boil. Add the peanut butter, tamari, molasses, pepper, garlic and lemon juice and stir until combined. Cook for 5 minutes, then remove from heat.

When the chicken is cooked, remove the pieces from the skewers and stir them into the sauce.

Serve the chicken and peanut sauce over a bed of brown rice, accompanied by Baked Bananas (page 131). Garnish with peanuts.

Chicken with Garden Vegetables ●

Makes 4 servings

2 chicken breasts, boned and skinned
1 tablespoon olive oil
1½ cups Low-Sodium Chicken Stock (page 52)
1 medium zucchini
2 medium ripe tomatoes
1 onion
1 garlic clove
2 tablespoons minced fresh parsley
2 teaspoons dried basil
2 teaspoons tamari

Cut the chicken breasts into bite-size pieces. Place them in a large skillet with the oil and saute until golden brown.

Place the stock in a deep ovenproof casserole. Halve the zucchini and cut into thin slices. Add to the stock.

Peel the tomatoes and remove the seeds. Chop them and add to the casserole. Chop the onion and add it along with the garlic, pushed through a garlic press or minced, the parsley, basil and tamari.

Add the chicken pieces to the casserole and stir together. Cover and bake in a preheated 350°F oven for 45 minutes. Serve over brown rice for a filling meal.

Variation: Add a finely chopped fresh hot pepper to the casserole for a spicy lift. Increase garlic to 3 cloves.

Chicken and Endive au Gratin ●

Endive adds a unique flavor to chicken, which is further complemented by the cheese sauce.

Makes 6 servings

2 chicken breasts, boned and skinned
1 egg white
1 tablespoon cornstarch
6 large Belgian endives
1 lemon
2 tablespoons olive oil
3 tablespoons butter
2 tablespoons whole wheat flour
1¾ cups milk
1 cup shredded Gruyere or Swiss cheese

Cut the chicken into large bite-size pieces. Beat the egg white slightly. In a medium bowl, toss the chicken with the cornstarch until the chicken is coated. Add the egg white and toss again. Set aside in a cool spot.

Cut the endives in half lengthwise and squeeze some lemon juice over the cut surfaces. Place in a steaming basket over boiling water. Steam about 5 minutes, or just until slightly tender. Spread the endives out to cool.

Place the oil in a large skillet. Saute the chicken pieces over medium-high heat, stirring often, until they are opaque throughout and lightly browned.

Remove the centers of the endive halves by carefully cutting out the bottom, where the leaves are attached. Remove the centers in one piece, leaving three or four outside leaves (hollowed halves) to fill with chicken.

Place the hollowed endive halves in a shallow baking dish. Divide the chicken pieces among the endive halves. Invert the endive centers over the chicken.

To make the cheese sauce, melt the butter in a medium skillet. Stir in the flour, then continue to stir for 2 to 3 minutes, to lightly cook the flour.

Stir in the milk, then continue to stir over medium heat until the sauce thickens. Stir in the shredded cheese, and as soon as it begins to melt, remove from heat.

Spoon the cheese sauce over the stuffed endives, covering them completely. Bake in a preheated 350°F oven for about 25 minutes, or until the endives are tender. Before serving, place under a broiler to lightly brown the top.

Slow-Baked Ginger Chicken

Makes 4 servings

2 chicken breasts, halved, boned and
   skinned
1 tablespoon Ginger Juice (this page)
1 tablespoon sesame oil
1 tablespoon sunflower oil
2 teaspoons tamari
1 garlic clove
1 small onion
2 scallions (garnish)
   parsley sprigs (garnish)

Place the chicken breasts between two sheets of waxed paper. Using a mallet, pound them until they are about ¼ inch thick.

Combine the ginger juice, oils, tamari and garlic, pushed through a garlic press, in a small bowl. Place some of this mixture in the bottom of a shallow ovenproof casserole.

Cut the onion into thin slices, then place a layer of onions on the bottom of the casserole.

Add the chicken pieces in one layer and spoon the remaining ginger mixture over them. Tightly cover the casserole with foil.

Bake in a preheated 325°F oven for 1½ hours. Garnish with the scallions, cut into thin, 3-inch strips, and parsley. Serve over brown rice, accompanied by broccoli and a salad.

Ginger Juice— A Snap to Make

Some people dislike biting into a hidden piece of pungent ginger root. But you can add the flavor of ginger, and bypass its pungency, by using ginger juice.

To prepare it, first grate the root, using the medium or fine holes of a grater. Place the grated ginger root on a square of cheesecloth and gather up the edges to form a bag. Twist the cheesecloth around the ginger to press out the juice. One-quarter cup of grated ginger will yield about 2 tablespoons of ginger juice, which can be used to flavor marinades and enhance the flavor of stir-fry dishes.

Chicken Livers with Red Pepper and Onion

Makes 2 servings

 1 pound chicken livers
½ sweet red pepper
 1 small onion
 2 tablespoons olive oil
 2 teaspoons tamari
   minced parsley (garnish)
   red pepper rings (garnish)

Rinse the chicken livers and cut them in half to make bite-size pieces.

Cut the pepper into thin, 1-inch-long strips. Slice the onion into thin rings.

Place the oil in a medium skillet and cook the pepper and onion rings over low to medium heat until firm-tender.

Add the chicken livers. Cook, turning the livers, until they are firm throughout and the juices are clear.

Stir in the tamari and remove from heat. Garnish with parsley and pepper rings and serve with brown rice or pilaf.

Chicken Veronique

● ● ●

A lovely dinner for guests—pretty but not difficult to prepare.

Makes 4 servings

 1 chicken breast, halved, boned and
   skinned
 1 tablespoon safflower oil
 1 tablespoon butter
 1 small red onion, chopped
 1 tart red apple, cubed
⅔ cup apple juice
 2 teaspoons arrowroot
 1 cup seedless red grapes
 2 tablespoons minced fresh parsley
   dash of ground nutmeg
 2 cups hot cooked brown rice

Cut the chicken meat crosswise into ½-inch strips. Place the oil in a large skillet, and when the pan is warm, add the butter. Place the chicken strips in the pan when the butter has melted.

Cook the chicken over medium heat until opaque throughout. Remove from the pan with a slotted spoon so the oil and juices remain in the pan.

Add the onions and apple cubes to the pan. Stir over medium heat until the onions are translucent. Add the apple juice and simmer until the onions are tender, about 10 minutes.

Add the arrowroot and stir over low heat until the sauce has thickened slightly. Stir in the grapes and chicken and heat through.

Stir in the parsley and nutmeg, then serve over brown rice.

Chicken Pilau with Currants ●

Delicately seasoned brown rice accompanies chicken and vegetables in one satisfying dish.

Makes 4 servings

 1 large onion, chopped
 2 tablespoons sunflower oil
 4 chicken thighs, skinned
1¾ to 2 cups Low-Sodium Chicken
   Stock (page 52)
¼ teaspoon saffron
⅛ teaspoon ground cinnamon
½ cup dried currants
 3 carrots, sliced diagonally
½ cup uncooked brown rice

Place the onions and oil in a large saucepan and cook over low to medium heat until translucent. Add the chicken thighs and cook over medium heat until they are lightly browned.

Add ¾ cup of stock, the saffron and cinnamon. Reduce heat, cover and simmer for 15 minutes. Stir in another cup of stock, the currants, carrots and rice.

Bring the ingredients to a boil, then reduce heat, cover and simmer for 45 minutes. Stir and add an additional ¼ cup of stock if the mixture seems dry. Turn off heat and keep covered for 10 minutes before serving.

Chicken Livers with Fennel and Currant Brown Rice ●●

This recipe provides an exciting new way to prepare a very economical ingredient—chicken livers.

Makes 4 servings

1½ cups uncooked brown rice
  3 cups Low-Sodium Chicken Stock
    (page 52)
 ½ cup dried currants
  8 to 10 scallions, sliced diagonally
    dash of ground allspice
1½ pounds chicken livers
  1 cup chopped onions
  1 cup chopped fennel
  2 tablespoons sunflower oil
  2 tablespoons tamari
    minced fresh parsley (garnish)

In a medium saucepan, place the rice, stock, currants, scallions and allspice. Bring to a boil, then reduce heat and simmer for about 4 minutes. Stir.

    Cover and turn the heat as low as possible. Steam the rice for about 40 minutes, then turn off heat and allow it to stand for another 10 minutes before serving.

    When the rice is nearly done, prepare the chicken livers. Halve or quarter them to make generous bite-size pieces.

    In a large skillet, place the onions, fennel and oil. Stir over medium heat until tender.

    Add the chicken livers and cook until the livers are just slightly pink inside. Stir in the tamari and remove from heat. Serve over the brown rice and garnish with parsley.

Find chicken livers ordinary? Try them cooked with fennel and served over savory brown rice with currants. It's an extra-ordinary treat.

Roasted Game Hens

●●

Plan on using a 1¼-pound hen for each serving.

Makes 4 servings

4 Cornish game hens or squabs
¼ cup Butter-Half (page 133)
2 small onions, halved
8 whole cloves
1 orange, peeled and sectioned
3 bunches watercress (garnish)
    orange slices (garnish)

Rinse the game hens and pat dry. In a large skillet, melt the butter. Add the game hens and cook over medium to high heat until browned on all sides, 3 to 4 minutes.

Place an onion half, stuck with two cloves, in the cavity of each game hen, along with some orange sections. Tie the legs together with string.

Place the game hens on a rack in an open roasting pan. Using a piece of cheesecloth that is large enough to cover the game hens, absorb the butter remaining in the skillet. Drape this cheesecloth over the game hens.

Bake in a preheated 375°F oven for 35 to 45 minutes, or until a leg moves easily in its socket.

Arrange the watercress, stems toward the center, around the edge of a serving platter. Remove the cheesecloth covering, then remove the onion and orange segments. Place the game hens on the serving dish and garnish with orange slices.

Enchiladas con Pollo ●●

The special flavor of fresh coriander permeates the filling.

Makes 4 servings

1 chicken breast, halved, boned and
    skinned
2 small onions, finely chopped
½ stalk celery, finely chopped
3 tablespoons corn oil

1 tablespoon minced fresh coriander
½ teaspoon Homemade Chili
    Seasoning (page 87) or chili
    powder
1 egg
1 tablespoon skim milk
2 cups Hot Chili Sauce (page 86)
8 corn tortillas
½ cup shredded cheddar cheese
1 cup Sour Yogurt-Cream (page 132)
½ cup scallions, sliced diagonally
3 radishes, thinly sliced

In a small saucepan, place the chicken in water to cover. Bring just to the boiling point, then reduce heat, cover and poach until tender, about 45 minutes.

Meanwhile, place the onions, celery and oil in a large skillet and cook over medium heat until the onions are translucent and begin to get tender. Stir in the coriander and chili seasoning and reduce heat to low.

Beat the egg with the milk and add to the skillet. Stir occasionally to scramble the egg and remove from heat as soon as it is set.

When the chicken is tender, remove from heat and drain, saving the liquid for soup stock. Cube the chicken and combine with the egg mixture.

To assemble the dish, place some of the chili sauce in a small skillet. Bring it to a boil, then reduce heat to simmer.

Dip the tortillas, one at a time, in the chili sauce, just long enough to soften the tortillas, about 30 seconds. (If the tortillas cook too long, they will fall apart: They should be just flexible.)

As each tortilla is ready, place it on a work surface, top with some of the chicken mixture and roll it up. In a shallow 9 × 13-inch baking dish place the tortillas seam-side down, forming a row.

Pour the remaining chili sauce over the tortillas and sprinkle with cheese. Cover the baking dish loosely with foil.

Bake in a preheated 350°F oven for 30 minutes. Remove from the oven and spoon the sour yogurt-cream down the center of the row of enchiladas. Sprinkle with scallions and radishes. Serve hot.

Each of these dishes is healthful and just right for entertaining. Use chicken to stuff Enchiladas con Pollo or wrap it up for Dijon chicken in Phyllo. For an impressive main dish, stuff some Roasted Game Hens.

Chicken Legs Stuffed with Herbed Mushrooms

These flavorful chicken legs are boned and stuffed with an herbed mushroom filling.

Makes 4 servings

   8 chicken legs
   3 tablespoons butter
   4 scallions, finely chopped
1½ cups chopped mushrooms
  ⅓ cup dry whole wheat bread crumbs
  ¼ teaspoon dried marjoram
   1 tablespoon sunflower oil
   3 tablespoons minced fresh parsley

With a boning knife or other small sharp knife, separate the chicken from the bone at the thigh end. Using the knife, gently scrape down the bone to separate the chicken, without cutting into the meat. (This process will turn the leg meat inside out.) Cut around the bone at the bottom to separate the meat from the bone.

Turn the chicken leg right side out. Remove and discard skin.

To prepare the stuffing, melt half the butter in a medium skillet. Add the scallions and cook over low heat until they wilt. Stir in the mushrooms. Cook until the mushrooms have released their liquid and it has evaporated.

Stir in the bread crumbs and marjoram. Remove from heat. Divide the stuffing among the boned chicken legs. Fill the openings of the chicken with stuffing, closing the meat around it.

Arrange the stuffed chicken legs in a shallow 9-inch baking dish. Cover loosely with a piece of cheesecloth. Dot the cheesecloth with the remaining butter.

Bake in a preheated 350°F oven for 1 hour, basting several times. When the chicken legs are done, carefully remove the cheesecloth, then pour the drippings from the baking dish into a small saucepan.

Add the oil and set over low heat. Stir in the parsley, and remove from heat as soon as the parsley has wilted.

Serve over brown rice pilaf with some of the parsley sauce spooned over each stuffed chicken leg.

Dijon Chicken in Phyllo ●

A wonderful dish for a buffet dinner: The filling will stay warm longer because it is wrapped in layers of phyllo.

Makes 6 servings

Filling
  ⅓ cup whole wheat flour
   1 teaspoon dried thyme
  ⅛ to ¼ teaspoon cayenne pepper
   2 chicken breasts, halved, boned
      and skinned
   2 tablespoons olive oil
   2 tablespoons unsalted butter
   4 shallots, finely chopped
   1 cup sliced mushrooms
   2 tablespoons heavy cream
   4 teaspoons Dijon-style mustard
   1 tablespoon minced fresh chives
Phyllo Wrapping
12 sheets phyllo pastry
  ⅓ cup olive oil
  ⅓ cup butter

To make the filling, combine the flour, thyme and pepper on a large, flat plate. Cut the chicken into bite-size pieces and coat with the flour mixture.

In a large skillet, heat the oil slightly and add the butter. When the butter has melted, stir in the shallots. Stir until translucent, about a minute.

Add the chicken pieces, in one layer. (If the skillet cannot hold all of the chicken, cook it in two batches.)

Turn the chicken and cook until golden on all sides. Remove the chicken and shallots and scrape up any meat that clings to the pan.

Mix-and-Match Poultry Stuffings

Select your favorite ingredients from columns A, B and C. Bind them together with some beaten egg or moisten them with milk. Use for stuffing poultry or fish.

A	B	C
Boiled potatoes	Chopped dates	Chopped leeks
Bread crumbs	Chopped prunes	Chopped onions
Bread cubes	Cranberries	Diced celery
Brown rice	Diced apples	Diced peppers
Bulgur	Dried apricots	Minced shallots
Cornbread	Dried currants	Mushrooms
Ground nuts	Raisins	Parsley and herbs
Wild rice	Sunflower seeds	Shredded carrots

Add the mushrooms to any oil remaining in the pan. Add a few drops of water, if necessary, to prevent scorching. Cook until the mushrooms have released their liquid and it has evaporated.

Return the chicken and shallots to the pan. Stir together the cream and mustard, then stir this into the chicken mixture. Heat through, until the sauce around the chicken thickens. Remove from heat and stir in the chives.

To prepare the wrapping, place the oil in a small saucepan. Cut the butter into pieces and add to the oil. Cook over low heat until the butter has melted.

On a work surface, lay out one sheet of phyllo pastry at a time. (Keep the other sheets wrapped in waxed paper until ready to use.) With a pastry brush, moisten half of the sheet with the oil and butter mixture. Fold the sheet in half.

Place some of the chicken filling 3 inches from one end of the phyllo.

Fold the end of the phyllo over the filling. Fold the edges up toward the center to contain the filling.

Roll the remaining dough around this filled section and place seam-side down on a lightly oiled baking sheet. Brush the top lightly with the oil and butter mixture. Repeat with the remaining phyllo leaves.

Bake in a preheated 350°F oven for about 20 minutes, or until the rolls are golden brown. Serve hot, accompanied by brown rice pilaf and steamed vegetables, and a fresh fruit dessert.

Variation: For *Dijon Chicken with Brown Rice,* replace the heavy cream with 1 cup of light cream. Stir it into the chicken with the mustard. Served over cooked brown rice, this makes four servings. (Of course, the phyllo wrapping is completely eliminated in this variation.)

Chicken lends itself to a variety of salad choices. Here, from left, it is marinated with mint for Minted Chicken Salad; complemented with the Oriental flavor of coriander in Chinese Chicken Salad; or mixed with rice in Main Dish Chicken Salad.

Peggy's Chinese Chicken Salad ● ●

This version is not your every-day chicken salad.

Makes 4 servings

Marinade
 1 tablespoon raisins
 ¼ cup water
 1 teaspoon honey
 1 teaspoon tamari
 3 tablespoons safflower oil
 1 tablespoon sesame oil
 1 tablespoon lemon juice
 ¼ teaspoon ground coriander
Salad
 1 chicken breast, halved, boned
     and skinned
 1 teaspoon safflower oil
 1 teaspoon sesame oil
 2 oranges
 ½ head romaine lettuce
 ¼ cup chopped fresh coriander, or
     to taste
 5 scallions, sliced diagonally

To prepare the marinade, place the raisins and water in a small skillet. Bring to a boil, then reduce heat and simmer until the raisins are soft and the water has evaporated.

Place the raisins in a blender with the honey, tamari, oils, lemon juice and coriander. Process on low speed until smooth, then place in a medium bowl.

To prepare the salad, cut the chicken into thin strips about 2 inches long. Saute the chicken in the oils just until cooked, about 5 minutes. Place the chicken in the marinade and refrigerate until chilled, about 10 minutes.

Peel the oranges and cut into sections, peeling off the membrane. Tear the lettuce into large pieces.

Place the orange sections, lettuce, coriander and scallions in a serving bowl. Add the chicken and marinade and toss.

NOTE: The chicken for this recipe may be prepared ahead. Simply marinate overnight, then combine with the other ingredients.

Minted Chicken Salad ● ●

Makes 4 servings

 3 cooked chicken breast halves,
     boned and skinned
 ¼ cup minced fresh mint
 2 tablespoons minced fresh parsley
 ⅔ cup rice vinegar
 2 tablespoons sunflower oil
 1 tablespoon honey
 1 ripe pineapple

1 cup seedless grapes
   red leaf lettuce
2 kiwi fruits (garnish)
   mint sprigs (garnish)

Cut the chicken breasts into thin strips about 2 inches long. (There should be 3 to 3½ cups.) In a medium bowl, combine the chicken with the mint, parsley, vinegar, oil and honey. Toss gently.

Cover the bowl tightly and refrigerate overnight, or at least 4 to 5 hours.

Cut the pineapple in half lengthwise, and set one half aside for later use. Cut the remaining piece in half again lengthwise. Remove the core and peel deeply enough to eliminate the eyes.

Cut the pineapple into spears ¼ to ½ inch thick and 2 inches long. Gently toss the marinated chicken, pineapple and grapes together.

Arrange the red leaf lettuce on individual salad plates or a serving plate. Arrange the chicken salad on the lettuce.

Peel and slice the kiwi fruits. Garnish the salad with the kiwi slices and mint sprigs.

NOTE: This delicate dish requires a mild vinegar such as rice vinegar, which is available in Oriental and health food stores. If, however, you must use a strong vinegar, reduce the amount to ⅓ cup and increase the oil to 3 tablespoons.

Main Dish Chicken Salad ●

Use both white and dark chicken meat for best taste.

Makes 6 servings

3 cups chopped cooked chicken
1 cup cooked brown rice
1 cup seedless grapes
½ cup finely chopped celery
½ cup Whole-Egg Mayonnaise
   (page 48)
¼ teaspoon ground coriander
¼ teaspoon dried marjoram
¼ teaspoon dried basil
18 large leaves spinach
3 kiwi fruits (garnish)
1 hard-cooked egg (garnish)

Place the chicken, rice, grapes, celery, mayonnaise, coriander, marjoram and basil in a large bowl. Fold together gently with a wooden spoon.

Place three spinach leaves on each serving plate. Top with a mound of chicken salad.

Peel and slice the kiwi fruits. Arrange around the chicken salad on each serving plate.

Press the egg yolk and egg white separately through a sieve. Garnish each mound of chicken salad with some of the white and yolk. Chill, if desired.

9

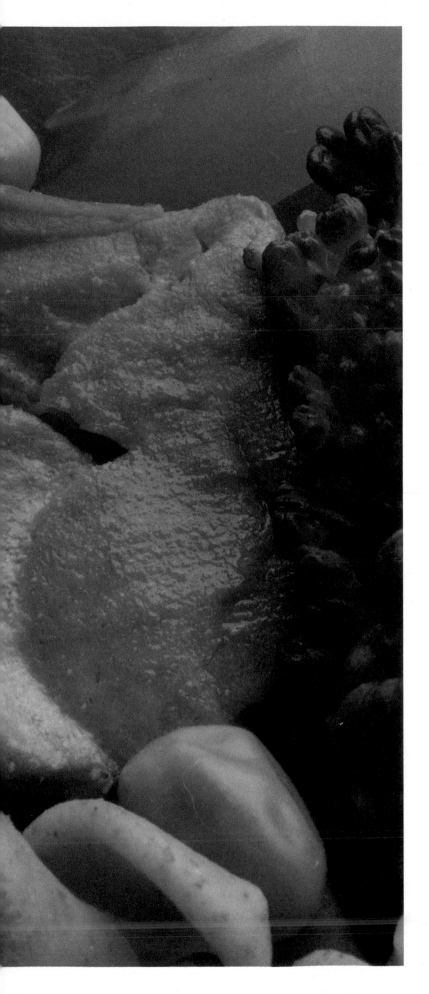

Fresh, Fabulous Fish

Stuffed, spiced or topped with sauce, fish is good food. High in protein, often low in fat, it lends itself to many dishes.

Most of the meat in our diet isn't wild anymore. Steers spend part of their lives in "feed lots," putting on extra fat. Chickens are kept nearly immobile to grow fat faster. That's why fish is such a treat—it's *natural* meat, bred by Mother Nature.

For instance, fish is low in calories; it contains about two-thirds the calories found in an equal serving of red meat. (Even a fairly skimpy broiled hamburger weighs in at about 290 calories, while an equal serving of swordfish has only 174.)

Most fish is low in fat, too. And the fat it contains can be a special kind, a type of polyunsaturate scientists call "omega-3." This fat (found in salmon, mackerel, trout, haddock and sardines) fights against heart disease by changing the chemistry of the blood so that it's less likely to form artery-clogging clots.

Fine, you say. But what about all that *salt?* Isn't it an invitation to high blood pressure? Fish—even ocean fish—is actually fairly low in salt—and packed to the gills with many good minerals.

But what if a broiled fish fillet doesn't set your taste buds quivering? Dive into this chapter! These fish recipes are exciting as well as healthful. Consider Mako Shark and Vegetable Kabobs, Paella, Fruit-Topped Perch Fillets and Chilled Poached Tuna with Strawberry-Garlic Mayonnaise to tempt your taste buds.

Fish isn't just for Friday anymore. It's good any day of the year and any time of the day. It can be a nutritious light lunch or an intriguing breakfast or brunch, as well as a superb dinner dish. After trying these unusual, healthful seafood dishes, you'll be glad you took up fishing.

Flounder with Lemon Broccoli ● ● ●

Simple, elegant and absolutely delicious.

Makes 4 servings

  2 large stalks broccoli
  1 lemon
  1 pound flounder fillets
  1 tablespoon sunflower oil
  1 tablespoon butter
  2 tablespoons whole wheat flour
  ¾ cup skim milk
  ½ cup shredded cheddar cheese
     lemon slices (garnish)
     parsley sprigs (garnish)

Cut the florets (tops) of the broccoli from the stalks, saving the stalks for another use. Separate the florets. Steam just until slightly tender, about 5 minutes.

Meanwhile, finely grate some of the rind from the lemon and then squeeze out the juice.

When the broccoli is done, cool it under cold running water. Sprinkle with the lemon juice and a little lemon rind, to taste.

Wrap the flounder fillets around the broccoli florets with the stems toward the center of the fillets. Place the flounder rolls seam-side down in a shallow baking dish.

To make the cheese sauce, place the oil and butter in a small skillet. When the butter has melted, add the flour and stir over low heat for 2 or 3 minutes.

Add the milk and stir over low heat until the sauce has thickened. Next, add the cheese, but stir only until the cheese begins to melt. Then remove from heat and continue to stir until the cheese has melted completely.

Pour the cheese sauce over the fish. Bake in a preheated 350°F oven for 25 minutes, or until the fish is opaque and baked throughout.

Serve from the baking dish, garnished with lemon slices and parsley.

At the Fish Market

When you purchase whole fish, look for bright, clear and prominent eyes, bright red gills and firm flesh with tight scales. Do not buy fish with cloudy, sunken eyes, pinkish-gray or brown gills or flesh that looks dull and dried out. Also keep away from any seafood with a "fishy" odor. Truly fresh fish have a mild and slightly briny aroma.

Haddock Souffle

Many people know haddock as *the* fish to deep-fry. This souffle, however, shows the fish's more subtle qualities of flavor.

Makes 4 servings

  1 cup skim milk
  ½ pound haddock fillets
  2 tablespoons butter
  1 teaspoon minced shallots
  2 tablespoons whole wheat flour
  ⅓ cup finely grated carrots
  1 tablespoon minced fresh parsley
     dash of freshly grated nutmeg
  4 egg whites
  2 egg yolks

Place the milk in a small skillet and bring just to the boiling point. Add the haddock fillets and poach just until opaque throughout, about 5 minutes.

Remove the fish from the skillet. Allow the fillets to cool slightly, then flake them. Reserve the milk.

Melt the butter in a small saucepan. Stir in the shallots, and when they are translucent, add the flour. Stir over medium heat for a minute or two.

Add the reserved milk and stir until the sauce has thickened slightly. Add the carrots and simmer 2 to 3 minutes. Remove from heat and stir in the flaked fish and parsley.

Place the egg whites in a large bowl and beat with an electric mixer on low, then medium speed until they form stiff peaks.

When the carrot mixture has cooled slightly, stir in the egg yolks. Gently fold about one-fourth of the carrot mixture into the beaten egg whites. Then gently fold in the remaining carrot mixture.

Pour the mixture into a lightly oiled 1¾-quart souffle dish and bake in a preheated 325°F oven until puffed and golden, 35 to 40 minutes. Serve at once, topped with Tomato Sauce (page 116) and accompanied by brown rice pilaf and steamed broccoli.

Almond-Baked Flounder ●

Makes 4 servings

1 egg, beaten
2 tablespoons skim milk
8 flounder fillets (about 1½ pounds)
⅓ cup wheat germ
⅓ cup ground almonds
¼ cup grated Parmesan cheese
¼ cup bran
    lemon slices (garnish)
    dill sprigs (garnish)
    carrot curls (garnish)

Combine egg and milk. Dip the flounder fillets into the mixture.

In a small bowl, stir together the wheat germ, almonds, cheese and bran. Place the mixture on a large plate and dredge the coated fish.

Arrange the fish in one layer on a lightly oiled shallow baking pan. Bake in a preheated 350°F oven for 10 minutes, or until the fillets are opaque throughout.

Place the baked fish on a warm serving plate. Garnish with lemon slices topped with dill sprigs and carrot curls. Serve hot.

Marinated Bluefish in Parchment ● ●

Wrapping is a perfect method of keeping fish hot for an indoor or outdoor buffet. Let each guest unwrap the fish at the table.

Makes 4 servings

⅔ cup orange juice
2 tablespoons tamari
¼ cup grated peeled apples
¼ cup grated onions
½ teaspoon grated orange rind
1½ to 2 pounds bluefish fillet
4 teaspoons sesame seeds
8 thin orange slices
4 scallions

To prepare the marinade, combine the orange juice, tamari, apples, onions and orange rind in a shallow dish large enough to hold the fish in

one layer. Cut the bluefish fillet into four serving pieces.

Place the fish in the marinade, spooning some over the top. Cover tightly with foil and marinate for 1 to 2 hours in the refrigerator.

To prepare the fish for baking, cut four pieces of parchment paper about twice the size of the pieces of fish. Lightly oil the paper.

Place one serving of fish on each piece of parchment, along with a little of the marinade. Sprinkle with a teaspoon of sesame seeds and top each piece with two overlapping orange slices.

Cut the scallions to approximately the length of the fish pieces. Leaving about an inch of the stem end to hold the scallion together, cut the green tops of the scallions into thin, lengthwise strips. Place one on each serving of fish.

Wrap the fish in the parchment, crimping the edges to seal. Place on a baking sheet and bake in a preheated 375°F oven for 18 minutes.

NOTE: Aluminum foil can be used in place of parchment paper.

Flounder with Lemon Broccoli sets the tone for a dinner party. Rely on its elegance and the knowledge that the dish is tasty and nutritious.

Chilled Poached Tuna with Strawberry-Garlic Mayonnaise ●

Once you've tried poached, fresh tuna, you'll not be tempted by the canned variety again. This is an elegant dish with an unusual sauce.

Makes 2 servings

```
1 thick lemon slice
2 bay leaves
¾ to 1 pound tuna steak
    Boston lettuce leaves
½ cup Strawberry-Garlic
    Mayonnaise (page 49),
    chilled
4 whole strawberries with caps
    (garnish)
```

Place enough water in a medium saucepan to cover the fish. Squeeze the juice from the lemon slice into the water, then add the slice to the pan. Add bay leaves and bring just to the boiling point over medium heat.

Slip the tuna steak into the pan and reduce the heat as the water nears the boiling point. (The water should shiver but not bubble.)

Poach 10 minutes for each inch of thickness and test to see that the center is opaque. Remove from heat and drain.

Remove any skin from the tuna and divide into two serving pieces. Cool, then chill the fish.

To serve, arrange lettuce leaves on each serving plate. Top with some of the tuna, then spoon mayonnaise over the fish. Garnish the side of each plate with a whole strawberry.

NOTE: Used as an appetizer, this dish serves four. Use a 1-pound tuna steak and divide into four serving pieces.

Grilled Swordfish Steaks ●

Makes 4 servings

```
2 large swordfish steaks (1 inch thick;
    about 1 pound each)
⅔ cup orange juice
2 tablespoons olive oil
2 teaspoons tamari
1 teaspoon maple syrup
1 teaspoon dried oregano
½ teaspoon finely grated orange rind
2 garlic cloves, halved
1 bay leaf
    orange slices (garnish)
    mint sprigs (garnish)
```

Place the fish in a shallow baking dish. To make the marinade, combine the orange juice, oil, tamari, maple syrup, oregano, orange rind, garlic and bay leaf. Pour over the fish. (If a blender is used to mix the marinade, add the garlic and bay leaf after blending.)

Cover tightly and refrigerate several hours or overnight, turning the fish once or twice.

Place the fish on a grill 3 to 4 inches from the hot coals. Grill 3 to 4 minutes on each side, or until the fish is cooked throughout. Baste occasionally with the marinade.

Arrange the fish on a serving platter. Garnish with orange slices and mint sprigs and serve, accompanied by a brown rice pilaf.

Fish Alternatives

These fishes are interchangeable in most recipes:

Sole — — Flounder — — Fluke

Cod — — Haddock — — Pollock

Bluefish — — Sea Trout — — Mackerel

Mako Shark — — Fresh Tuna — — Swordfish Steaks

Monkfish — — Lobster

Mako Shark and Vegetable Kabobs

Marinated mako shark has a flavor and texture that complements an assortment of zesty vegetables.

Makes 4 servings

1¼ pounds mako shark steaks
½ cup safflower oil
¼ cup tamari
¼ cup lemon juice
1 tablespoon minced peeled ginger root
2 garlic cloves, sliced
1 teaspoon grated orange rind
2 scallions, minced
2 large carrots
3 medium zucchinis
2 green or sweet red peppers
8 large mushrooms
⅔ cup olive oil
2 tablespoons tarragon vinegar
2 garlic cloves, minced
½ teaspoon Dijon-style mustard
½ teaspoon dried basil
½ teaspoon dried oregano
¼ teaspoon dried marjoram
¼ teaspoon dried rosemary
⅛ teaspoon freshly ground black pepper

Remove the skin from the shark steaks and cut the meat into generous bite-size cubes. To prepare the shark marinade, combine the safflower oil, tamari, lemon juice, ginger, sliced garlic, orange rind and scallions.

Place the shark cubes and marinade in a shallow glass dish. Cover tightly and refrigerate several hours or overnight.

Cut the carrots into ¾-inch-thick slices. Cut the zucchini into 1-inch slices. Cut the peppers into bite-size squares. Trim the stems from the mushrooms until they are even with the cap. (Save the stems for stock.)

To prepare the vegetable marinade, combine the olive oil, vinegar, minced garlic, mustard, herbs and pepper.

Cook the carrots in a small amount of water until they are crisp-tender, about 5 minutes. Steam the zucchini, peppers and mushrooms 1 minute.

Place the cooked vegetables in a shallow glass dish and add the marinade. Allow vegetables to cool slightly, then cover tightly and refrigerate several hours or overnight.

To prepare the kabobs, drain and discard marinade from the fish. Drain and reserve marinade from the vegetables.

Thread the shark cubes and vegetables alternately on four sturdy metal skewers. Place on a grill or under a broiler, turning often and basting with the reserved vegetable marinade. Cook 10 to 15 minutes, or until the vegetables are tender and the shark is cooked throughout.

Mako shark is a tasty alternative to higher-priced fish and offers the opportunity to try an unusual and delicious new food. Kabobs make good use of this firm-fleshed fish.

Seafood Tabbouleh

An elegant main dish salad suitable for the buffet.

Makes 8 servings

  1 cup bulgur
  1 cup water
  ½ cup lemon juice
  1 pound shrimp
1½ cups water
  1 lemon slice
  4 or 5 coriander seeds
  ½ pound lump crabmeat
  1 cup minced fresh parsley
  ½ cup minced fresh mint
  1 pint cherry tomatoes
  3 tablespoons virgin olive oil
  3 tablespoons sunflower oil
  4 scallions, sliced diagonally
  1 teaspoon fresh marjoram or ½
      teaspoon dried marjoram
  mint sprigs (garnish)

Place the bulgur, water and lemon juice in a medium bowl and set aside to soak.

In a medium saucepan, poach the shrimp in simmering water to which the lemon slice and coriander seeds have been added. Remove the shrimp, allow to cool slightly, then peel and devein.

Chop the shrimp, saving three or four for garnish. Pick over the crabmeat, removing any cartilage.

Assemble the salad in a large bowl, tossing together the soaked bulgur, chopped shrimp, crabmeat, parsley, mint, cherry tomatoes, oil, scallions and marjoram. Chill, tightly covered with foil. Before serving, garnish with the reserved shrimp and the mint sprigs.

Paella ● ● ●

Makes 8 servings

6 cups Garden-Vegetable Chicken Stock (page 53)
1 large onion, peeled
½ teaspoon saffron
1 sweet red pepper
2 cups uncooked brown rice
1 bay leaf
2 chicken breasts, halved, boned and skinned
½ pound medium shrimp
½ pound sea scallops
4 small lobster tails
½ cup olive oil
1 medium onion, chopped
4 garlic cloves, minced
1 tablespoon lemon juice
1 cup peas
2 tablespoons minced flatleaf parsley
  lemon wedges (garnish)
  parsley sprigs (garnish)

Place the stock, whole onion and saffron in a large saucepan. Bring to a boil, cover and reduce heat. Simmer 20 minutes, then turn off heat. Remove onion and discard, or save to add to another dish.

While the stock simmers, place the pepper directly over a gas burner, turned as low as possible, or under a broiler. Turn the pepper occasionally, until the outside is charred in places and the pepper begins to soften. Wrap the pepper in a damp kitchen towel and set aside.

Add the rice and bay leaf to the stock. Bring to a boil, cover and reduce heat to lowest possible setting. Steam the rice for 35 minutes, then set aside, still covered. Do not uncover the pan once the rice begins to steam.

Pound the chicken pieces between two pieces of waxed paper until they are uniformly ¼ inch thick. Cut into 2-inch strips. Pat dry.

Peel and devein the shrimp and cut the scallops into quarters. Cut the lobster tails in half lengthwise. Unwrap the pepper and carefully peel all of the skin from the flesh. Cut into 1-inch strips.

Place the olive oil in the paella pan and set over medium heat. When the oil is hot but not smoking, add the chicken strips. Quickly saute until golden, turning often. Remove the chicken from the pan with a slotted spoon and set aside.

Add the chopped onion to the oil. Reduce heat and stir until the onion is translucent. Add the garlic, shrimp, scallops, lobster tail halves and pepper strips. Continue to stir for another 3 to 4 minutes, until the lobster and shrimp begin to turn pink.

Remove the shrimp and lobster from the pan. Remove the bay leaf from the rice and place the rice in the pan. Add the lemon juice, peas and minced parsley. Stir to combine.

Bury the chicken and partially bury the shrimp in the rice. Decorate the paella with the lobster halves, shell-side up then place it in a preheated 325°F oven for 20 minutes.

Remove pan from oven and cover with foil. Allow to stand 10 minutes before serving. Garnish with lemon wedges and parsley sprigs. Serve with a green salad.

Variation: Five ounces of imported pimientos, diced, can be substituted for the sweet red pepper.

Add crabmeat and shrimp to a basic Middle Eastern salad and you have a Seafood Tabbouleh that will please your guests. Garnish with whole shrimp for buffet elegance.

Fresh Salmon Salad with Pesto ●

Worthy of center stage in a summer buffet.

Makes 8 to 10 servings

1 pound salmon steaks
2 lemon slices
1 pound whole wheat spiral noodles
1 large bunch broccoli
4 carrots
1 cup peas
1 large stalk celery
½ cup Pesto Sauce (this page)
⅓ cup sunflower oil
    grated Parmesan cheese

To a large skillet half filled with simmering water, add the salmon steaks and lemon slices. Poach the fish, with the water just below the simmering point, until it is cooked throughout, about 10 minutes. Remove, drain and set aside to cool.

Place the noodles in a large pot of boiling water. Return to the boil, then cook just until firm-tender. Drain the noodles in a colander, then cool them under cold running water.

Cut the broccoli florets from the stalks and cut the stalks on the diagonal. Quarter or halve the florets into large bite-size pieces.

Cut the carrots diagonally into thin slices, then place them in a steaming basket over boiling water. Steam 3 to 4 minutes, then add the broccoli and peas. Steam an additional 3 to 4 minutes, until all of the vegetables are crisp-tender. Cool under cold running water.

Cut the celery in half lengthwise and trim off the leaves. Slice thinly on the diagonal.

Remove the skin and bones from the cooled salmon steaks. Flake the fish and place it in a large bowl with the noodles and vegetables.

Combine the pesto sauce and oil in a small bowl. Spoon the pesto mixture over the salad and toss gently. Chill. Sprinkle with Parmesan cheese before serving.

Pesto Sauce ●

Makes 1½ cups

⅓ cup virgin olive oil
⅓ cup sunflower oil
⅔ cup unsalted pistachios
 2 garlic cloves
¾ cup freshly grated Parmesan cheese
 2 cups tightly packed fresh basil
 1 cup tightly packed watercress
        leaves

Place the oils, pistachios and garlic, pushed through a garlic press, in a blender or food processor. Process on medium speed until the mixture is combined, but the pistachios are just coarsely chopped.

Add the cheese and process on medium speed until combined.

Add the basil and watercress and process again, stopping to scrape down the sides as necessary, until the mixture is nearly smooth. Do not overprocess.

NOTE: The pesto can also be prepared in a mortar and pestle. Grind the nuts and garlic together until smooth. Add the cheese, then add the basil and watercress, a little at a time, with the oils. Add additional oil for a thinner pesto.

Variations: Substitute pine nuts or walnuts for all or part of the pistachios. Use only olive oil for total amount of oil. Use flatleaf parsley in place of the watercress, or eliminate watercress and add an additional cup of basil.

Fruit-Topped Perch Fillets ● ●

Apples, grapes, oranges and bananas complement perch fillets.

Makes 4 servings

1 cup apple juice
2 shallots, minced
1 apple, thinly sliced
1½ pounds perch fillets, with skin on
1 cup red seedless grapes
2 oranges, peeled and sectioned
1 banana, sliced diagonally
  dash of freshly grated nutmeg
3 cups hot cooked brown rice
1 tablespoon arrowroot
  minced fresh mint (garnish)

Place ¾ cup of the apple juice, the shallots and the apples in a large skillet. Bring to a boil, then reduce heat and simmer about 5 minutes, uncovered.

Add the perch fillets, in one layer, if possible, over the apples. Cover the pan and slowly simmer about 5 minutes.

Top the fish with grapes, orange sections and banana slices. Top with a dusting of nutmeg. Cover the pan and heat the fruit through.

Remove the fish and fruit carefully from the skillet with a spatula and arrange over cooked brown rice. Keep warm.

Mix together the remaining ¼ cup of apple juice and the arrowroot. Add to the juices in the pan and cook over medium heat until slightly thickened. Pour over the fruit and fish, and serve.

A special treatment for white fish—which is sweet but somewhat bland—is the addition of fruit. The apples, oranges, bananas and grapes complement the fish visually and add extra fiber and vitamin C.

Fish Facts

For really fresh fish, try catching your own. Fishing is satisfying on many levels. You'll enjoy the fresh sea air, the thrill of the catch, the peace that comes along with a day on the open water. And you'll especially marvel at how wonderful a truly fresh fish tastes. Cook your catch before sundown, and you'll never forget the tender, sweet flavor. If you want to do more than just pan-fry the fish, review the recipes in this chapter for some new approaches to preparing seafood.

Boning Fish Fillets

Most fish fillets are free of bones except for a row about one-third of the way back from the head end (wide end) of the fillet. These bones—there might be 8 or 10—are easily removed after the fish is cooked. Two exceptions are shad and pike. Fillets cut from these two kinds of fish may have "floating" bones, which are difficult to detect but easy to remove once they have been located.

Good News for Shellfish Lovers

Because of their presumed high cholesterol content, shellfish have usually been excluded from diets for prevention or treatment of high cholesterol levels in the blood. However, recent research has revealed that two groups of shellfish each have a different effect on blood cholesterol levels. While crab, shrimp and lobster remain suspect in their effect on cholesterol levels, clams, oysters and scallops are being given a clean bill of health. In fact, it looks like these mollusks can be compared to fish in regard to their effect on cholesterol levels. So, even if you are keeping a watchful eye on your cholesterol, you probably can still enjoy clams, oysters and scallops in reasonable amounts. (Check with your doctor if you are on a special diet.) Just be certain that they are well cooked. Otherwise you'll be flirting with hepatitis A or gastroenteritis. And try to be sure that your shellfish come from reputable dealers and are culled from nonpolluted waters. With a few precautions, you can eat and enjoy nutritious shellfish.

10

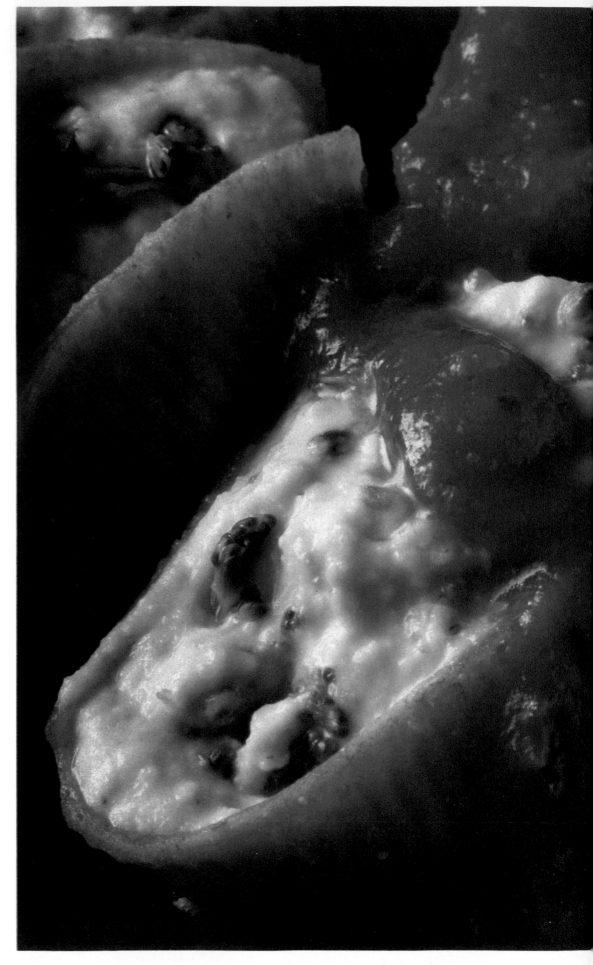

Hearty Vegetarian Feasts

This selection of main dishes brings you the world of nutritious, meatless meals.

D o vegetarians live longer? Anyone who's had an unimaginative serving of beans and rice might answer, "It only seems that way."

But vegetarian fare doesn't have to be dull. We've devised some of the most interesting meatless recipes you'll ever prepare. Moreover, they also may stir up your interest in vegetarian cuisine—an interest that usually leads to better health.

The fact is, numerous scientific studies have shown that vegetarians enjoy better health than those who eat meat. Seventh-Day Adventists, for example, who avoid eating meat and also refrain from smoking and alcohol, have significantly lower incidences of cancer, heart disease, high blood pressure and other ailments than the general population.

But we also know that health statistics rarely stimulate the appetite. If you don't like what you're eating, even the promise of better health won't motivate you enough to prepare that meal again. The "eat it, it's good for you" philosophy often collapses when faced with a menu that's less than mouth-watering. Recognizing that likelihood, we've concocted dishes that are both healthy and luscious.

So sit back. First, imagine yourself in Greece. There you'd find Spanakopita, an ethnic variety of spinach pie. It combines the flavors of butter, feta cheese and spinach, wrapped in a crusty shell of phyllo pastry. Dream of sunny Italy with your own Patio Pizza. Or visualize a pie filled to overflowing with a colorful combination of carrots, peppers, cauliflower, parsley and three cheeses. The dish, Golden Mountain Vegetable Pie, looks and tastes wonderful.

Spanakopita ● ● ●

Greek to you? In English, it means spinach pie, but it's a pie like no other.

Makes 8 servings

2 pounds spinach
1 large onion, finely chopped
¼ cup virgin olive oil
1 cup chopped scallions
½ cup minced fresh parsley
1 tablespoon minced fresh dill
¼ teaspoon freshly ground nutmeg
¾ cup crumbled feta cheese
¾ cup creamed cottage cheese
¼ cup freshly grated Parmesan
    cheese
4 eggs, beaten
12 sheets phyllo pastry
⅔ cup Butter-Half (page 133),
    melted

Remove large stems from spinach leaves and rinse the leaves very well. Chop coarsely, then steam them above boiling water just until wilted. Drain in a colander, pressing out any liquid with the back of a spoon.

Place the onions and oil in a large skillet. Cook over medium heat until the onions are slightly tender. Add the scallions and cook until limp. Remove from heat and stir in parsley, dill and nutmeg.

To the skillet, add the spinach, cheeses and finally the eggs, stirring gently.

To assemble the spanakopita, begin by brushing a shallow 9 × 12-inch baking dish with some of the butter-half. Fit one sheet of phyllo in the bottom of the dish, letting the edges drape over the rim. Brush with a little of the butter-half. Repeat with four more sheets.

Spread the spinach filling in the phyllo-lined dish. Top with remaining sheets of pastry, each brushed with butter-half.

Trim the excess phyllo, leaving about an inch around the edge of the baking dish. Roll the edge, making a lip around the top of the spanakopita. Chop the phyllo trimmings into "flakes," and coat with any remaining butter-half. Sprinkle the flakes over the top of the spanakopita.

Bake in a preheated 350°F oven for 45 minutes, until puffed and golden. Allow to cool at room temperature for about 10 minutes before cutting into serving pieces.

Variation: Substitute ½ pound of kale for ½ pound of the spinach. Chop it fine. Steam the kale slightly longer than the spinach. Substitute ⅓ cup virgin olive oil plus ⅓ cup melted butter for the butter-half.

Pierogi ● ●

Pierogi, with their high-quality protein, make an excellent main dish.

Makes 6 servings

4 potatoes, peeled and cubed
2 cups unbleached flour
1 cup whole wheat flour
1 egg
¾ cup water
1 medium onion, finely chopped
½ stalk celery, finely chopped
3 tablespoons sunflower oil
2 to 3 tablespoons hot milk
1 cup shredded sharp cheddar cheese
¼ cup butter

Place the potatoes in a large saucepan of water, bring to a boil, reduce heat and simmer until tender.

In a medium bowl, combine the flours and egg and enough of the water to make a stiff dough. On a lightly floured surface, roll the dough out ⅛ to 1/16 inch thick. Cut into 3-inch circles with a cookie cutter or rim of a drinking glass.

Set aside 2 tablespoons of the onions. In a small skillet, combine the remaining onions and the celery with the oil. Cook over low heat until tender. Turn off heat.

When the potatoes are cooked, pour off the water. Add some hot milk and mash the potatoes slightly. Add the onion and celery mixture, continuing to mash. Stir in the cheese.

Bring a large pot of water to a boil.

To prepare the pierogi, place some of the potato filling in the center of each dough circle. Fold the circles in half and crimp the edges

together with the tines of a fork.

Place the pierogi, several at a time, in the boiling water and boil for 2 to 3 minutes, or until the pierogi float to the surface. Drain well.

Melt the butter in a large skillet. Add the reserved onions and cook over medium heat until translucent.

Add the pierogi and continue to cook over medium heat until the

pierogi and onions are lightly browned. Serve hot, over steamed cabbage leaves.

NOTE: If the pierogi are to be frozen, prepare and boil; drain well, cool and freeze. To reheat, place in a pot of boiling water again, and complete recipe procedure.

The combination of cheese and eggs packs protein into this delicious Middle Eastern spinach pie. The filling is nestled between layers of delicate phyllo pastry.

Patio Pizza ● ● ● ●

Earthy and elegant, these pizzas are perfect for informal occasions, entertaining your guests indoors or out.

Makes 4 10″ pizzas

Crust
1¼ cups skim milk
  2 tablespoons active dry yeast
  1 teaspoon honey
  3 tablespoons sesame tahini
  1 tablespoon corn oil
  2 cups whole wheat flour
1½ cups unbleached flour
    stone-ground cornmeal
Toppings
  4 cups Tomato Sauce (this page)
  2 cups shredded mozzarella cheese
    thinly sliced tomatoes
    cooked sliced mushrooms
    steamed chopped spinach
    lightly steamed chopped green or
      sweet red peppers
    uncooked Marinated Tofu
      Triangles (page 120)

To make the crust, heat the milk in a small saucepan until lukewarm. Place the milk in a large bowl, stir in the yeast and honey and set aside. When the yeast mixture is foamy, stir in the tahini and oil.

Add the whole wheat flour and just enough unbleached flour to hold the dough together. Knead the dough on a lightly floured surface until it is smooth and shiny, about 15 minutes, or use a large mixer with a dough hook.

Place the dough in a large, lightly oiled bowl and turn to oil all sides. Cover and allow dough to rise in a warm place until doubled in bulk.

Punch down the dough and divide into four pieces. Knead each piece, then flatten the pieces into rounds about 6 inches across. Roll out to 10-inch circles. Fold up the rim of each circle to help contain the pizza sauce and toppings.

Sprinkle a baking sheet with cornmeal and lift dough for one pizza onto sheet. Pour ¾ cup of tomato sauce over the dough, spreading it evenly.

Sprinkle with ¼ cup of cheese. Arrange choice of toppings on the pizza, then sprinkle with another ¼ cup of cheese.

Let pizza rest for 10 to 15 minutes. Meanwhile, preheat oven to 500°F. Bake one pizza at a time, placing each on the lowest shelf or the floor of the oven for just 8 to 10 minutes, until the crust is golden. Repeat preparation and baking procedure for remaining pizzas, keeping the baked pizzas warm. Cut each into 4 slices before serving.

Variation: For nonvegetarian pizza, add cooked, crumbled ground beef or flaked tuna to the toppings.

Tomato Sauce ●

Makes 1 quart

  6 large garden-ripe tomatoes,
      quartered, or 4 cups Italian
      plum tomatoes with juice
  2 large sweet red peppers, seeded
      and coarsely chopped
  1 medium onion, quartered
⅔ cup tomato paste
¼ cup virgin olive oil
  3 garlic cloves
  2 teaspoons minced fresh basil or
      ½ teaspoon dried basil
  2 teaspoons fresh oregano or
      ½ teaspoon dried oregano
  1 teaspoon fresh marjoram or
      ¼ teaspoon dried marjoram
    dash of cayenne pepper (optional)

Place half of the tomatoes, half of the peppers and onions, the tomato paste, half of the oil and the herbs and cayenne in a blender. Process on low to medium speed until smooth, stopping to scrape down the sides as necessary.

Pour the blended sauce into a large saucepan. Repeat the blending process with the remaining tomatoes, peppers, onions and oil, and add this mixture to the saucepan.

Bring the sauce to a boil over medium heat, cover the pan and reduce heat. Simmer for 40 minutes, stirring occasionally.

NOTE: Prepare several quarts of sauce when harvest time arrives and freeze it for later use.

Cheese Dishes

Gruyere

Gruyere is a cured cheese made from whole cow's milk. It has a slightly sharper flavor than Swiss cheese, which it resembles.

Mozzarella

Traditionally made from buffalo's milk, mozzarella is now made from cow's milk. Sometimes called pizza cheese, it is soft and mild, melts easily and is most often used in cooking.

Feta

Feta, a traditional food in the mountains of Greece, is made from the milk of ewes or goats. In the United States, less flavorful versions are made from cow's milk. Feta is relatively high in sodium and should be used in small quantities for flavor.

Cheshire

English Cheshire has a stronger, more salty taste than its close neighbor, cheddar. Its distinctive flavor allows a little Cheshire to go a long way.

Cheshire Corn Souffle ●

The special tang of Cheshire cheese lifts this golden corn souffle straight out of the ordinary!

Makes 4 servings

    1 cup corn kernels
    ¾ cup skim milk
    2 tablespoons butter
    2 tablespoons whole wheat flour
        dash of ground nutmeg
    ¼ cup finely crumbled Cheshire cheese
    4 eggs, separated
        grated Parmesan cheese

Place ¾ cup of the corn along with the milk in a blender or food processor and process on medium speed until smooth. With a sharp knife, coarsely chop the remaining corn.

Melt the butter in a large saucepan, then add flour. Stir over low heat for 2 to 3 minutes.

Add the chopped corn, the blended corn mixture and the nutmeg. Turn heat to medium and stir frequently until the mixture thickens.

Stir in the Cheshire cheese, reduce heat to low and stir another 2 to 3 minutes. Remove from heat.

Beat the egg whites with a wire whisk or with an electric mixer on low, then medium speed, until they form stiff peaks.

When the corn mixture has cooled slightly, stir in the egg yolks. Gently fold in about one-fourth of the beaten egg whites to lighten the mixture. Then very gently fold in the remaining egg whites.

Butter a 2-quart souffle dish and dust the inside with Parmesan cheese. Carefully pour the souffle mixture into the dish.

Place the souffle in a preheated 400°F oven, turn the heat down immediately to 325°F, and bake for 35 minutes. Don't open the oven while the souffle is baking, or it may fall.

Serve immediately upon removing from the oven, while it is still puffed.

Variations: Substitute an equal amount of finely crumbled feta cheese for the Cheshire. Substitute ⅓ cup shredded sharp cheddar or Swiss cheese for the Cheshire.

Golden Mountain Vegetable Pie ● ●

A craggy congregation of cheeses and vegetables towering over a tender, tasty crust. Nice for a special occasion.

Makes 8 servings

Crust
1¼ cup whole wheat flour
    ½ cup butter
    ½ cup cottage cheese
    1 to 2 tablespoons cold water
Filling
    4 to 5 carrots
    2 medium sweet red peppers
    1 large cauliflower
    1 tablespoon minced fresh parsley
    1 cup crumbled feta cheese
    ¼ cup cottage cheese
    1 cup shredded mozzarella cheese

To make the crust, place the flour in a large bowl or in a food processor fitted with the steel blade. Use a pastry blender, or quick on-and-off turns of the processor, to cut the butter into the flour.

Use a fork, or several more quick on-and-off turns of the processor, to add the cottage cheese and enough of the water to make a smooth dough.

Flatten the ball of dough slightly, wrap in plastic wrap and refrigerate for 30 minutes.

To make the filling, cut the carrots into julienne strips. Cut the peppers into thin strips about 2 inches long. Separate the cauliflower into small florets. Cut the larger florets in half.

Place the carrots in the bottom of a large steaming basket. Add the cauliflower and pepper strips. Set over boiling water, covered, for 5 to 8 minutes, or just until the vegetables begin to get tender.

Place the cauliflower and peppers in a large bowl. Add the feta and cottage cheeses and toss well to combine.

Roll out the dough and place it in the bottom of a 9-inch pie plate. Place the carrot strips in the bottom of the crust, then top with the cauliflower and cheese mixture and sprinkle with the mozzarella cheese.

Bake in a preheated 350°F oven for 30 minutes, or until the cheese topping and crust are golden brown and the vegetables are tender.

Remove from the oven and allow to stand for about 5 minutes before cutting.

Variations: Substitute 1 cup shredded Swiss or Gruyere cheese for the mozzarella. Substitute ¼ cup ricotta cheese for the cottage cheese.

Broccoli- and Cheese-Stuffed Shells ● ● ●

Makes 4 servings

¾ pound jumbo whole wheat shells
2 cups ricotta cheese
1 cup cottage cheese
1 egg, beaten
3 tablespoons wheat germ
2 teaspoons Ginger Juice (page 91) dash of ground nutmeg
1 cup chopped cooked broccoli
12 large cabbage leaves

Bring a large pot of water to a boil. Add the shells and cook until firm-tender. Remove from heat, drain and cool under cold running water. Separate the shells.

To make the stuffing, combine the cheese, egg, wheat germ, ginger juice and nutmeg. Gently fold in the broccoli.

Stuff the shells with the cheese mixture. Line a shallow 9 × 12-inch baking dish with six large cabbage leaves. Arrange the stuffed shells over the cabbage. Cover with the remaining cabbage leaves.

Bake in a preheated 350°F oven for 20 minutes, or until the shells are heated through. If desired, serve with Tomato Sauce (page 116) on the side.

Macaroni and Cheese Orlando ● ●

After you have a taste of macaroni and cheese with this vegetable combination, you won't want it any other way!

Makes 4 servings

1 cup chopped broccoli
1 red pepper, cubed
2 cups whole wheat macaroni
2 tablespoons butter
2 tablespoons whole wheat flour
2 cups skim milk
1½ cups shredded sharp cheddar cheese
2 tablespoons grated Parmesan cheese

Steam the broccoli and pepper just until firm-tender, about 8 minutes. Set aside.

Cook the macaroni until firm-tender. Drain.

Meanwhile, make the sauce. Melt the butter in a medium skillet, then add the flour and stir over low heat 2 minutes.

Add the milk and stir over medium heat until the sauce begins to thicken slightly.

Layer the vegetables, macaroni and cheddar cheese in a deep 2-quart ovenproof casserole. Pour the sauce over top. Sprinkle with Parmesan.

Bake in a preheated 350°F oven for 40 minutes. Serve hot.

Cheddar
Cheddar is a hard cheese ranging in color from creamy white to deep yellow. It is made from whole cow's milk, and because of its relatively high sodium and fat content, it should be used rather sparingly.

Ricotta
Made from the whey of cow's milk, ricotta is a very soft and mild cheese. Whole or skim milk is added to this cheese, but it is low in fat and an excellent choice for dieters.

Parmesan
A very hard cheese, Parmesan is usually grated and used for flavoring. When fully cured, Parmesan keeps almost indefinitely and can be hand-grated when needed.

Swiss
Nutlike and slightly sweet, Swiss cheese is distinguished by the holes that develop as the cheese matures. It is relatively high in fat and should be used sparingly.

119

Tahini-Baked Cauliflower

Whole cauliflower baked in a whole wheat-tahini crust makes an impressive dish.

Makes 8 servings

1 large head cauliflower
1 cup sliced mushrooms
4 scallions, chopped
1 tablespoon sunflower oil
⅔ cup whole wheat flour
½ cup sesame tahini
¾ cup water
2 tablespoons tamari
   parsley sprigs (garnish)

Steam the cauliflower for 20 minutes. Meanwhile, cook the mushrooms and scallions in a small skillet with the oil, stirring often, until the scallions are tender.

In a medium bowl, combine the flour and tahini. Stir in the water and tamari thoroughly to make a batter.

Pour just enough of the batter into a lightly oiled 8-inch baking pan or pie plate to cover the bottom. Sprinkle with the mushrooms and scallions.

Center the cauliflower in the baking pan and spoon the remaining batter evenly over it.

Bake in a preheated 350°F oven for 20 minutes. Garnish with parsley. Cut into pie-shaped wedges to serve.

Marinated Tofu Triangles ●

The tofu becomes more flavorful the longer it marinates.

Makes 4 servings

1 pound tofu
¼ cup grated peeled ginger root
2 garlic cloves
2 tablespoons tamari
1 tablespoon sesame oil
4 scallions, chopped

Cut the tofu into approximately ¼-inch slices. Arrange, in one layer, if possible, in a shallow 9 × 13-inch dish.

To make the marinade, place the ginger on a piece of cheesecloth. Push the garlic through a garlic press directly onto the ginger. (The garlic can also be minced.)

Wrap the cheesecloth around the ginger and garlic to make a little bag. Twist the cheesecloth to remove the juice from the ginger and garlic, letting it drip into a shallow bowl. (There should be about 2 tablespoons.)

Add the tamari and oil to the juice. Pour the marinade over the tofu and allow it to marinate, turning occasionally, anywhere from 15 minutes to several hours. (Cover with plastic wrap and refrigerate if the tofu is to marinate more than 30 minutes.)

Broil the tofu slices until they are lightly golden, then turn and broil the other side. Just before serving, cut each slice in two on the diagonal, to make triangles. Serve hot, garnished with scallions and accompanied by Leek Brown Rice Pilaf (page 139) and broccoli.

Spinach Lasagna
● ● ●

The traditional dish is fabulous, but loaded with calories. This alternative version of lasagna is light but just as fabulous.

Makes 6 servings

1 pound spinach
¾ pound whole wheat lasagna noodles
2 cups ricotta cheese
1 cup farmer's cheese
¼ cup freshly grated Parmesan cheese
2 eggs, beaten
   dash of freshly grated nutmeg
2 tablespoons butter
2 tablespoons whole wheat flour
1 cup milk
¾ cup shredded mozzarella cheese
1 cup Tomato Sauce (page 116)

Rinse the spinach, then remove and discard stems. Place in a large saucepan over medium heat until wilted. Drain well and press out liquid.

Bring a large pot of water to a boil. Add noodles and cook until firm-tender. Drain and rinse under cold water to separate the noodles.

While the noodles are cooking, combine the ricotta, farmer's and Parmesan cheeses, eggs and nutmeg in a large bowl. Chop the spinach and add it to the cheese mixture.

In a medium skillet, melt the butter and stir in the flour. Stir over low heat a minute or so, then add the milk all at once, stirring to eliminate any lumps. When the mixture has thickened, stir in the mozzarella. Remove from heat.

To assemble the lasagna, coat the bottom of a shallow 9 × 12-inch baking dish with a thin layer of tomato sauce.

Add a layer of noodles, then half of the spinach and cheese mixture. Top with another layer of noodles and the remaining spinach and cheese.

Add another layer of noodles and spoon the cheese sauce over top. Add a final layer of noodles and spoon the remaining tomato sauce over all.

Bake the lasagna, loosely covered with foil, in a preheated 350°F oven for 30 minutes. Remove from the oven and let stand about 10 minutes before cutting into serving pieces.

Carrot and Broccoli Quiche ● ● ●

Real men eat this quiche—and so do real women and children. Colorful and creamy, it's a delightful supper dish.

Makes 8 servings

Filling
1 cup diced carrots
1 cup diced, peeled broccoli stalks
1 cup chopped broccoli florets
1 medium onion, finely chopped

1 tablespoon butter
2 teaspoons whole wheat flour
3 eggs
¾ cup whole milk
   dash of ground nutmeg
½ cup finely diced Italian fontinella
      cheese
Crust
¾ cup whole wheat flour
2 tablespoons soy flour
2 tablespoons wheat germ
¼ cup corn oil
2 tablespoons buttermilk
Garnish
   dash of paprika
8 kale leaves
8 orange slices

To make the filling, steam the carrots for 7 minutes, the broccoli stalks for 5 minutes and the florets for 3 minutes, until the vegetables are firm-tender. (This can be done at one time: After the carrots have steamed for 2 minutes, add the broccoli stalks and in another 2 minutes, add the florets. Steam all the vegetables the remaining 3 minutes.)

Place the onions in a small skillet with the butter. Cook until just slightly tender. Stir in the whole wheat flour and cook an additional 2 to 3 minutes, stirring often. Remove from heat.

Place the eggs and milk in a blender and add nutmeg. Process on low to medium speed until smooth.

Stir the vegetables, onion mixture and cheese together in a medium bowl.

To make the crust, place the flours and wheat germ in the bottom of a 9-inch pie plate and stir to combine. Add the oil and buttermilk, and stir with a fork until moistened.

Press the pie shell against the bottom and sides of the pie plate. Press the top edge with the tines of a fork to make a decorative edge.

Place the vegetable mixture evenly in the pie shell. Pour in the egg mixture. Garnish with a light dusting of paprika. Bake in a preheated 350°F oven until firm, about 40 minutes. Serve hot or chilled. Garnish plates with kale and orange slices.

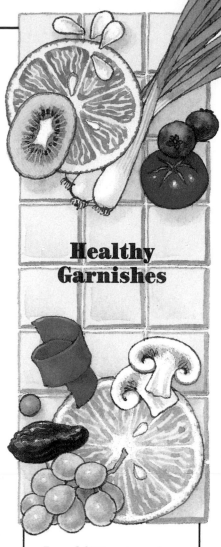

Healthy Garnishes

In addition to color, garnishes also can add a bit of flavor and nutrition. Consider using some of the following: mushrooms, grapes, kiwi slices, scallions, cherry tomatoes, lemon or lime slices, carrot curls, berries and the florets of cauliflower and broccoli.

Falafel Patties

These patties can serve as a main course for dinner, or as a change-of-pace lunch.

Makes 4 servings

¼ cup sesame tahini
2 tablespoons minced fresh parsley
1 tablespoon sunflower oil
1 tablespoon lemon juice
1 tablespoon tamari
1 teaspoon ground cumin
1 teaspoon ground coriander
½ teaspoon chili powder
1 egg
1 cup cooked chick-peas
¾ cup wheat germ
¼ to ½ cup yogurt, at room temperature
3 scallions, sliced diagonally
¼ cup alfalfa sprouts

Place the tahini in a blender with the parsley, oil, lemon juice, tamari, cumin, coriander, chili powder and egg. Process on low speed until smooth.

Add the chick-peas and blend at low speed until smooth, stopping to scrape down the sides of the container as necessary. Place the mixture in a medium bowl.

Stir in the wheat germ. Form the falafel mixture into four patties, or eight small patties if they are to be used in pita sandwiches.

Cook the patties in a lightly oiled skillet, turning when the bottom is golden. To serve, top each with a tablespoon or more of yogurt, some of the scallions and sprouts.

NOTE: To make sandwiches, allow one pita bread per serving. Slice down the middle to make two half-pie shapes, then open the "pocket." Place a small falafel patty in each, spoon on some yogurt and add chopped scallions and sprouts.

Variation: Add some chopped tomatoes to the topping.

Vegetarian Burgers

Delicious hot or cold.

Makes 4 servings

2 cups grated carrots
1 medium onion, finely chopped
2 eggs, beaten
¾ cup sunflower seeds
¾ cup cooked chick-peas
1 tablespoon chopped fresh parsley
¼ teaspoon ground cumin
¼ teaspoon ground coriander
dash of ground allspice

In a large bowl, combine the carrots, onions and eggs. Place the sunflower seeds in a blender or food processor fitted with the steel blade and process with short bursts until ground. Add to the carrot mixture.

If you use a blender, grind small amounts of the chick-peas until mealy, or process in the processor with the steel blade until thoroughly mashed.

Add the chick-peas, parsley, cumin, coriander and allspice to the carrot mixture and stir together until well combined. Chill until firm. Form into patties.

This quartet of hearty vegetarian dishes crosses national boundaries. From left: Vegetarian Burgers, made with chickpeas, and open-faced mozzarella cheese sandwiches are both rather American. Falafel Patties combine sesame seeds and chickpeas for Middle Eastern flavor. And, of course, quick-as-a-wink Pita Pizza, combining wheat bread and cheese, had its beginnings in romantic Italy.

Cook the patties in a large oiled skillet, turning when lightly browned. Serve with Tomato Sauce (page 116), if desired, or in Plain Whole Wheat Rolls (page 27).

NOTE: If serving patties in sandwiches, spread the rolls with Whole Egg Mayonnaise (page 48) and add chopped tomatoes, lettuce, sprouts and a grinding of black pepper.

Mozzarella Broil with Asparagus

Makes 2 servings

 4 stalks asparagus
 2 whole wheat English muffins,
     cut in half
 ½ teaspoon soft butter
 2 slices tomato
 2 thin slices mozzarella cheese
 6 cherry tomatoes (garnish)
 2 orange slices (garnish)
     mint sprigs (garnish)

Cut the asparagus into pieces about 5 inches long. Discard tough bottoms. Steam just until firm-tender, then cool under cold running water. Set aside.

Spread the muffins with a thin layer of butter. Toast lightly under a broiler. Set aside two of the muffin halves.

Place a tomato slice on each of the remaining muffin halves. Place under the broiler just a minute to heat through.

Place two asparagus spears on each tomato slice. Cover with the mozzarella and place under a broiler until the cheese melts.

Serve at once, open-faced, on plates garnished with cherry tomatoes, orange slices and mint.

Pita Pizzas

Makes 4 servings

 1 large onion, finely chopped
 1 medium sweet red pepper, finely
     chopped
 2 tablespoons corn oil
 1 cup sliced mushrooms
 ½ teaspoon dried marjoram
 ½ teaspoon dried basil
 ½ teaspoon dried oregano
 1 garlic clove, thinly sliced
 4 whole wheat pita breads
 ⅓ cup tomato paste
 4 very thin slices tomato
 4 thin slices mozzarella cheese
     alfalfa sprouts (garnish)

Place the onions and pepper in a large skillet with the oil. Stir over medium heat until the onions are translucent.

Add the mushrooms, herbs and garlic. Stir until the mushrooms have given up their liquid and the liquid has evaporated. Remove from heat.

Place the pita breads under a broiler and toast one side. Spread some tomato paste over the untoasted sides, then spread with the onion mixture.

Place a thin slice of tomato in the center of the pizzas, then top with the mozzarella. Broil just until the cheese has melted and is lightly browned. Garnish with sprouts.

Broccoli and Tofu Stir-Fry ● ●

Makes 4 servings

2 large stalks broccoli
3 tablespoons corn oil
2 medium onions, cut into thin strips
3 to 5 garlic cloves, thinly sliced
1 teaspoon minced peeled ginger root
1 pound tofu, cubed
   dash of cayenne pepper
2 to 3 tablespoons tamari
3 cups hot cooked brown rice

Cut the broccoli stalks from the florets, then peel the stalks and slice them thinly on the diagonal. Coarsely chop the florets. Set them aside separately.

Heat the oil in a wok or a large skillet over medium to medium-high heat until it is hot but not smoking. Stir in the onions and broccoli stalks. Stir constantly, until the onions are translucent. Add a few drops of water, as needed, to prevent sticking.

Stir in the garlic and ginger, stir a minute or so, then add the broccoli florets. Stir until the florets become a dark green.

Add the tofu, cayenne and tamari. Stir, then cover the pan so the vegetables and tofu can steam.

Remove from heat when the vegetables are just crisp-tender. Serve at once over hot rice.

NOTE: This recipe can be prepared quickly by using leftover brown rice heated in a steamer.

Oriental-style Broccoli and Tofu Stir-Fry complements brown rice for a high-protein meal. Serve with a light soup, with fruit for dessert.

Crepes

Despite their French name and gourmet mystique, crepes are really just thin pancakes. They're so adaptable, they can be served at almost any meal. Begin with a properly made crepe, then add whichever fillings or toppings suit your fancy.

Fillings

Cooked fish, shellfish or poultry

Cooked vegetables, creamed or plain

Scrambled eggs with dill

Stewed dried fruits

Chopped fresh fruits

Shredded cheeses

Ricotta cheese

Leftovers

Apple-Prune Butter (page 20)

Applesauce

Toppings

Sour Yogurt-Cream (page 132)

Tomato Sauce (page 116)

Maple Whipped Cream (page 151)

Cooked fish or poultry, creamed

Strawberry Sauce (page 20)

Honey-Apple Topping (page 21)

Carob-Maple Dessert Topping (page 158)

Sauteed mushrooms

Chopped fresh fruit

Lemon or orange rind, finely grated

Light Lunches

What comes to mind when you think "light lunches"? The same old soup or salad? The same old boring tuna? Well, *brighten* as well as *lighten* by trying these interesting luncheon alternatives. Each dish offers a serious serving of vitamins and minerals to satisfy your body, and each can be presented beautifully—to please your spirit, too. Try simple garnishes to add interest to light lunches. Orange, apple or pear slices, grapes, sprouts, herb sprigs and other fruit and vegetable tidbits are edible ornaments that add nutrients to your lunch without adding a lot of calories. The four dishes here also can be complemented with whole grain muffins or bread for extra fiber.

Scrambled Eggs Florentine

Makes 1 serving

½ teaspoon butter
1 cup loosely packed chopped
    spinach leaves
1 egg
1 tablespoon skim milk
1 tablespoon cottage cheese
    cherry tomatoes (garnish)

Melt the butter in an omelet pan or small skillet. Add the spinach and stir over low heat until the leaves are thoroughly wilted.

Beat the egg lightly in a small bowl, then beat in the milk. Pour over the spinach and stir over low heat until the egg is almost set.

Stir in the cottage cheese, and when the egg is cooked, remove to a serving plate. Add a couple of cherry tomatoes for garnish.

Variation: Substitute 1 tablespoon of finely crumbled feta cheese for cottage cheese.

Potato Frittata ●

Makes 2 servings

1 teaspoon butter
1 cup diced cooked potatoes
3 eggs
1 tablespoon minced fresh parsley
½ cup grated sharp cheddar cheese
    parsley sprigs (garnish)

Place the butter in a medium skillet and when it has melted, add the potatoes. Cook over medium heat until the potatoes are heated through and begin to brown.

Beat the eggs in a small bowl and add the parsley. Pour over the potatoes.

Allow the eggs to set without stirring. When the bottom of the eggs has cooked and they are just runny on top, sprinkle with the cheese and place under a broiler.

When the frittata has puffed and is golden and the cheese has melted, cut in half and serve, garnished with parsley sprigs.

Papaya-Lemon Omelet ●●

Makes 1 serving

2 eggs
1 teaspoon honey
½ teaspoon finely grated lemon rind
¼ teaspoon vanilla extract
½ teaspoon safflower oil
½ teaspoon butter
¼ ripe papaya, seeded and sliced
   watercress sprigs (garnish)

Beat the eggs with the honey, lemon rind and vanilla until well combined.

Heat an omelet pan or medium skillet, then add the oil and butter. When the butter has melted, add the egg mixture.

Cook over medium heat, pulling the edges of the omelet toward the center of the pan with a table knife. Swirl the pan to allow uncooked egg to reach edge of pan.

When the eggs have cooked so that they have just set on top, remove from heat. Lay two slices of papaya at the center of the omelet, then fold the eggs over the papaya and slide the omelet out of the pan onto a plate. Garnish with the remaining papaya slices and watercress.

Variation: Substitute ¼ cup sliced, ripe strawberries for papaya to make *Strawberry Omelet.*

Lemon Yogurt with Fruit ●●●

Makes 2 servings

1 cup Lemon Yogurt (page 17)
1 nectarine, cubed
1 cup strawberries, sliced
½ cup sliced bananas or red
   raspberries
4 to 6 small mint leaves
   mint sprigs (garnish)

Place the yogurt in a serving bowl. Gently fold in the fruit and mint leaves. Chill, if desired, and serve, garnished with mint sprigs and accompanied by whole grain muffins.

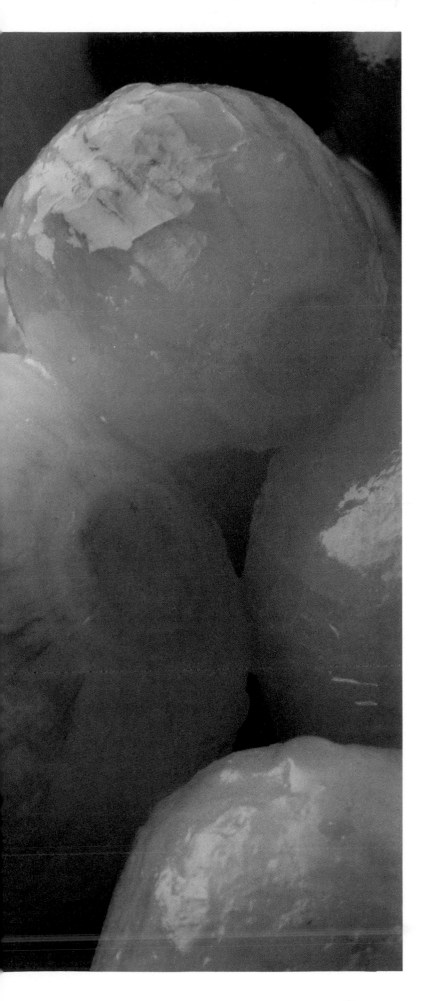

Dazzling Side Dishes

It's a shame to set them on the side. Imaginative and healthful, they add luster to any meal.

S ide dishes are traditionally served on the side, playing second fiddle to the meat. It's a shame because side dishes can be one of the main elements of a nutritious meal. Not only do they add interest and color, they can add serious nutrition, as well.

Fiber is one of the most important contributions of the vegetables and grains that accompany our main courses—especially if that main course is meat, chicken or fish. Fiber is that ever-vigilant maintainer of a healthy digestive tract.

In addition, vegetables and grains are jam-packed with vitamins and minerals that complement main dishes. Vegetables are particularly rich in vitamins A and C, as well as the B complex group. Grains are good sources of the minerals zinc, calcium, magnesium and potassium.

If your thoughts about side dishes are mired in mashed potatoes and peas, the side dish recipes in this chapter will pry them loose.

We'll have you setting the sideboard with Glazed White Onions with Seedless Grapes, Honey-Glazed Cherry Tomatoes, Pecan and Wild Rice Pilaf, and Fennel Provencal with Mushrooms. Anything but dull company for a serving of chicken, don't you think?

We'll help you prepare side dishes in a flash, too, when your schedule's cramped. For example, we advise doubling the amount of brown rice you prepare for one meal so that you'll have extra rice ready the next time you need it. Then you can either steam the rice or whip it up into a delicious pilaf in just a couple of minutes. We'll also help you cut down on the saturated fat in your favorite toppings. Want a clue? Turn to our suggestions for Sour Yogurt-Cream and Butter-Half. You'll be trimmer for it, too.

Corn Pudding Souffles with Cherry Tomatoes

Makes 4 servings

1½ tablespoons unsalted butter
 1 tablespoon whole wheat flour
 ¾ cup skim milk
 ⅔ cup corn kernels
 2 eggs
 2 tablespoons crumbled feta cheese
 ⅛ teaspoon freshly grated nutmeg
 4 cherry tomatoes
   dash of paprika (garnish)

Place the butter in a medium saucepan over low heat. When it has melted, stir in the flour. Continue stirring for another 2 to 3 minutes over low heat. Do not allow the flour to brown.

Add the milk and stir to eliminate lumps. Bring to a boil over medium heat, then stir in the corn. Remove from heat when corn is heated through.

Place the corn mixture in a blender, hold down the lid and process on low, then medium speed until smooth.

Add the eggs, feta and nutmeg. Process again on low, then medium speed until smooth. (The corn mixture can also be placed in a food processor fitted with the steel blade, and pureed for 10 seconds until smooth. Then add the eggs and feta and process another 10 seconds until the eggs have been incorporated.)

Divide the blended mixture among four oiled baking ramekins or custard cups. Top each with a cherry tomato.

Place the ramekins or custard cups in a shallow baking pan filled with boiling water to a depth of ½ inch. Bake in a preheated 350°F oven for 30 minutes, or until the pudding souffles are puffed and golden. Sprinkle with paprika and serve immediately.

A light approach to corn. These souffles, flavored with feta cheese and garnished with cherry tomatoes, are dazzling additions to any meal.

Fennel Provencal with Mushrooms ●

If you haven't a favorite way with fennel, or if you've never tried it, this recipe is just for you!

Makes 2 servings

1 fennel bulb
1 tablespoon butter or olive oil
1 garlic clove, halved
1 large ripe tomato, peeled, seeded
   and chopped
½ cup sliced mushrooms
2 tablespoons Low-Sodium Chicken
   Stock (page 52)
½ teaspoon fresh thyme or ⅛
   teaspoon dried thyme

Cut off any feathery tops from the fennel bulb to use as garnish. Slice the fennel in half lengthwise, then cut lengthwise into thin strips.

In a medium skillet, melt the butter or heat the oil slightly. Add the garlic, stirring over low heat until it turns a light golden brown. Remove, if desired.

Add the fennel and tomatoes. Cover and simmer, stirring occasionally, for about 5 minutes.

Add the mushrooms, stock, and thyme. Simmer partially covered, stirring occasionally, for about 10 minutes, or until the vegetables are tender.

Remove cover and cook down any liquid that remains in the pan, until the vegetables are just moist. Serve hot, garnished with fennel sprigs.

Maple-Molasses Baked Beans ●●

A sweet and spicy mixture that's low in saturated fat because it's meatless.

Makes 8 servings

1 onion, finely chopped
1 green pepper, finely chopped
1 tablespoon corn oil
⅔ cup tomato paste
2 tablespoons blackstrap molasses
2 tablespoons maple syrup
1 tablespoon tamari
1 teaspoon chili powder
    dash of cayenne pepper
2 cups Vegetable Stock (page 53)
4 cups cooked navy or other white beans

In a large skillet, cook the onions and peppers in the oil. Add a little water if the mixture gets too dry.

Stir in the tomato paste, molasses, maple syrup, tamari, spices and stock. Bring to a boil.

Place the beans in a large ovenproof casserole and stir in the tomato sauce mixture. Cover and bake in a preheated 350°F oven for 1 hour.

Remove cover and bake about 30 minutes more, stirring once or twice.

Baked Bananas ●●

Serve with curries or as a side dish with Grilled Chicken with Peanut Sauce (page 90).

Makes 4 servings

4 medium ripe bananas
1 tablespoon butter
1 tablespoon lemon juice

Peel the bananas and halve them lengthwise. Arrange them in a shallow baking dish.

Serve Maple-Molasses Baked Beans as a hearty but healthy low-fat accompaniment to family dinners or picnic fare.

Dot the bananas with butter and sprinkle with lemon juice. Bake in a preheated 400°F oven for 6 to 8 minutes, or until they are soft. Gently remove to a serving platter or individual dinner plates. Serve hot.

Autumn Applesauce ●●

Makes 6 servings

4 cups diced apples
1 cup apple cider

Place the apples in a blender with the cider. Process on low, then medium speed until smooth.

Place the mixture in a medium saucepan. Bring to a boil over medium heat, then reduce heat, cover and simmer 15 minutes. Serve warm, or chill.

Variation: Add a dash of cinnamon, if desired. Use apple juice in place of cider.

Low-Cal Sour Yogurt-Cream

While plain yogurt is a good substitute for sour cream on baked potatoes and other dishes—and also a good way to cut back on saturated fat—some people miss the taste of sour cream. The solution to the dilemma is a yogurt/sour cream combination.

Stir together 1 cup plain yogurt and ½ cup sour cream. Use it to top potato pancakes, cooked vegetables or fresh fruit. Or add a dollop to soup.

If you plan to heat the mixture, add 1 tablespoon cornstarch to prevent it from separating.

Steamed Cabbage with Poppy Seeds ●

Very simple. Very good.

Makes 6 servings

1 medium head cabbage, coarsely shredded
2 tablespoons butter
1 teaspoon poppy seeds

Place the cabbage in a steaming basket or colander over boiling water. Steam for 7 to 10 minutes, or just until firm-tender.

In a large bowl, toss the cabbage with the butter. When the butter has melted, toss with the poppy seeds. Serve hot.

NOTE: Eliminate poppy seeds when serving steamed cabbage with pierogi.

Carrot Nests ●

Serve with fish dishes or chicken, accompanied by steamed broccoli or snow peas.

Makes 4 servings

4 medium carrots
2 tablespoons Butter-Half (opposite page)
2 tablespoons water
2 tablespoons Low-Sodium Chicken Stock (page 52)
 dash of ground cinnamon
 dash of ground nutmeg
 watercress sprigs (garnish)

Use a vegetable peeler to cut very thin, long shreds of carrot, ¼ to ½ inch wide. Reserve the tough centers of the carrot, which are harder to shred, for another recipe.

Melt the butter-half in a large skillet. Add the carrots and stir until they begin to stick. Add the water and stock at intervals, using just enough to prevent the carrots from scorching.

Dust with cinnamon and nutmeg, to taste, while cooking. Remove from the pan when the carrots are tender but still retain their shape.

Form into four mounds, or "nests" on a serving plate or on individual plates. Serve hot, garnished with watercress.

Variation: For a sweeter flavor, substitute apple juice for the chicken stock.

Glazed White Onions with Seedless Grapes ● ● ●

Serve with Roasted Cornish Game Hens (page 94), other poultry, or fish.

Makes 4 servings

10 to 15 small white onions
 2 tablespoons butter
½ cup white grape juice
 1 cup seedless grapes

Peel the onions. Melt the butter in a medium stainless steel or ceramic skillet. Add the whole onions and stir over low to medium heat until they are light golden brown.

Add the grape juice. Reduce heat, cover tightly and simmer over very low heat about 20 minutes, or until the onions are tender.

Add the grapes and stir until heated through. Remove the onions and grapes with a slotted spoon and set aside in a warm place.

Turn the heat up to medium-high and boil down the remaining liquid until it is reduced by about half. (There should be about 2 tablespoons of sauce.)

Stir the onions and grapes into the sauce until they are hot, then turn out into a serving bowl, or arrange them on a platter, surrounding a main course.

Sweet Potatoes with Apricots and Prunes

● ● ● ●

Makes 6 to 8 servings

4 medium sweet potatoes
⅓ cup pitted prunes
¼ cup dried apricot halves
2 cups apple cider
1 tablespoon butter

Cut the sweet potatoes into large cubes. Place in a medium ovenproof casserole with a lid.

Add the remaining ingredients. Push the prunes and apricots down so that they are in the liquid. Cover the casserole.

Bake in preheated 350°F oven for 1 hour, stirring once or twice during baking.

To serve, carefully drain the hot liquid from the casserole into a small saucepan. Keep the casserole hot as you boil down the liquid to half its volume over medium-high heat. Pour the sauce over the sweet potatoes and serve hot.

Butternut Squash, Scallion and Pineapple Casserole ●

Makes 6 servings

4 cups cubed butternut squash
4 to 5 scallions, chopped
1 tablespoon butter
1 cup cubed pineapple
¼ cup unsweetened pineapple juice
     or apple cider
   dash of ground nutmeg
¼ cup sunflower or pumpkin seeds
     (garnish)

In a small skillet, melt the butter over low heat. Add the scallions and cook, stirring often, until translucent.

Combine the squash, scallions and pineapple in a shallow baking dish. Pour the juice or cider over the squash and dust with nutmeg. Cover the dish tightly with foil.

Bake in a preheated 350°F oven for 45 minutes, then remove the foil, stir and bake an additional 15 minutes uncovered.

Toast the sunflower or pumpkin seeds on top of the stove or in the oven.

When the squash is tender, remove from the oven. Sprinkle with toasted seeds and serve.

Honey-Glazed Cherry Tomatoes ●

A quick and delightful side dish that fills in on buffets or fast meals, adding a good share of nutrition and color to the menu.

Makes 4 servings

1 tablespoon butter
2 cups cherry tomatoes
1 tablespoon honey
1 tablespoon minced fresh mint
     (garnish)

Melt the butter in a medium skillet. Add the cherry tomatoes and stir until heated through.

Drizzle the honey over the cherry tomatoes and stir until the tomatoes are coated. Remove from heat and place in a serving bowl. Garnish with mint.

Butter-Half

If you like the taste of butter but want to cut back on saturated fats, try this half-and-half combination that uses polyunsaturated oil. Butter-half spreads easily and can be used for baking and cooking.

To prepare 1 cup, bring ½ cup butter to room temperature. Place it in a blender or food processor along with ½ cup safflower oil and ⅛ teaspoon liquid lecithin. (The lecithin helps combine the oil and butter and prevents it from separating, but can be omitted, if necessary.)

Process these ingredients on low speed until thoroughly combined. Use a spatula to place the butter-half in a small crock or ramekin. Keep refrigerated.

Butter-half becomes softer at room temperature than whole butter, but this is an advantage. A smaller amount spreads farther on bread, toast or muffins, so you'll use less.

Ratatouille ● ●

Serve over Polenta (this page) as a vegetarian main dish. Top with grated cheese, if desired.

Makes 6 servings

3 tablespoons sunflower or olive oil
1 medium eggplant, cubed
2 small zucchinis, cubed
2 medium onions, chopped
2 sweet red peppers, cut into short
    strips
4 garlic cloves, minced
1 teaspoon fresh basil or ½ teaspoon
    dried basil
1 teaspoon fresh marjoram or ½
    teaspoon dried marjoram
1 teaspoon fresh oregano or ¼
    teaspoon dried oregano
3 tomatoes, coarsely chopped
¼ cup tomato juice or Low-Sodium
    Chicken Stock (page 52)
1 tablespoon tomato paste
1 teaspoon tamari
¼ cup minced fresh parsley
   grated cheddar or Parmesan
    cheese (optional)

Place 2 tablespoons of oil in a large skillet set over medium heat. Add the eggplant and stir until slightly tender. Remove from the skillet, set aside and keep warm.

Add the remaining oil to the skillet. Add the zucchini and cook over medium heat just until slightly tender. Add to the eggplant and keep warm.

Place the onions and peppers in the skillet. Add a few drops of water, if necessary, to prevent sticking, and cook over low heat until the onions are translucent and slightly tender.

Add the garlic and herbs. Cook until the onions are tender but not browned. Place the tomatoes over the mixture and cover the pan.

Cook over low heat for about 5 minutes, or until the tomatoes begin to release their juice. Uncover and stir, cooking off any excess liquid from the vegetables.

Layer the tomato mixture with the eggplant and zucchini in a deep ovenproof casserole. Combine the tomato juice or stock with the tamari and pour over the vegetables.

Cover the casserole and bake in a preheated 350°F oven for 20 to 25 minutes. Stir in parsley and serve hot. If desired, top with grated cheese.

Polenta ● ● ●

This dish may be served two ways—hot and creamy, or cut into cakelike squares.

Makes 6 to 8 servings

1½ cup stone-ground cornmeal
4½ cups water
  1 cup shredded sharp cheddar
    cheese (optional)
  2 tablespoons freshly grated
    Parmesan cheese (optional)

Stir together the cornmeal and 1 cup of cold water until combined, pressing out any lumps. Set aside.

Bring the remaining 3½ cups of water to a boil in a large saucepan. Stir in the moistened cornmeal, then stir immediately and rapidly with a wire whisk until the entire mixture returns to a boil.

Reduce heat and partially cover the pan. Simmer about 20 minutes, stirring frequently with the whisk.

To serve polenta hot and creamy style, stir in the cheeses and continue to stir until the cheddar has melted. Serve at once or keep hot in the top of a double boiler, if necessary, before serving.

To serve as squares, do not add the cheeses. Spread the warm polenta out in a lightly oiled, shallow 9 × 12-inch baking dish. Cool, then chill 3 to 4 hours or overnight.

To reheat polenta, cut into squares. Place on a baking sheet and heat in a preheated 400°F oven for about 15 minutes.

Polenta Squares with Cheese ● ● ●

Serve as a side dish with poached fish and steamed fresh vegetables.

Makes 10 to 12 servings

Polenta (opposite page), chilled and cut into squares
1½ cups shredded sharp cheddar cheese
¼ cup freshly grated Parmesan cheese

Carefully place the polenta squares on a lightly oiled baking sheet.

Combine the cheeses and pile some on top of each square.

Heat in a preheated 400°F oven until the cheese has melted and the polenta is heated through, about 15 minutes. Serve hot.

Variation: For *Ratatouille Polenta Squares,* place the polenta squares on a lightly oiled baking sheet. Heat for 10 minutes in a preheated 400°F oven. Top each square with a dollop of hot Ratatouille (opposite page) and bake an additional 5 minutes. Serve hot, with additional ratatouille in a serving dish on the side.

Cooked polenta, cooled and cut into squares, can be served a number of ways. Top with cheese or add ratatouille for an impressive company dish.

Wilted Romaine Lettuce with Garlic and Mushrooms

Blanched quickly in boiling water, romaine lettuce becomes an admirable and unusual side dish.

Makes 4 servings

3 tablespoons virgin olive oil
3 to 4 garlic cloves, thinly sliced
½ cup sliced mushrooms
4 teaspoons tamari
8 large leaves romaine lettuce

Bring a large pot of water to a boil.
Meanwhile, place the oil in a small skillet over low heat. Add the garlic and stir until slightly tender but not browned.

Stir in the mushrooms and continue to cook, stirring frequently, until the mushrooms have released their liquid and it has nearly evaporated.
Stir in the tamari and remove from heat. Keep warm.
Quickly dip the lettuce leaves in the boiling water and remove them as soon as they are wilted, about 3 to 5 seconds.
Arrange the lettuce on a serving plate. Drizzle the sauce over it and serve.

Green Beans with Almonds and Ginger ●

Makes 4 servings

1 pound green beans
2 tablespoons safflower oil
1 teaspoon minced peeled ginger
    root
½ teaspoon tarragon vinegar
½ teaspoon honey
¼ cup sliced almonds

Steam the green beans for 4 to 5 minutes, or just until crisp-tender. Place them under cold running water to stop further cooking.
Place the oil in a large skillet. Add the ginger, stirring over low heat a minute or two. Add the vinegar, honey and beans. Stir just until the beans are heated through.
Stir in the almonds and remove from heat. Serve hot.

Artichokes with Mustard Dip ● ●

When artichokes are in season, do enjoy them. But rather than using melted butter or hollandaise as a dip, try our cholesterol-free dressing.

Makes 4 servings

4 large artichokes
¼ cup virgin olive oil

If you want a different side dish for company meals, try Artichokes with Mustard Dip. The tang of the dip sets off the subtle flavor of the artichokes.

2 tablespoons lemon juice
1 teaspoon Dijon-style mustard

Bring a large pot of water to a boil. Meanwhile, trim the artichoke stems to within ½ inch of their bottoms. With a scissors, also trim the tops of individual leaves, if desired.

Place the artichokes in the boiling water and partially cover the pot. Reduce heat slightly and cook at a slow boil for 30 to 40 minutes, or until tender. Test with a sharp fork inserted into the stem end.

Drain thoroughly. Mix the oil, lemon juice and mustard for the dip in a small bowl. Divide among four individual baking ramekins or custard cups.

The artichoke is best eaten by pulling each leaf from the bulb, then dipping it into the sauce. Only the meaty flesh at the bottom of each leaf is eaten.

When the leaves have been removed, use a spoon or grapefruit knife to remove the prickly "choke" from the center of the artichoke. Cut up the remaining artichoke (the heart) and dip it into the mustard sauce.

Carrot and Sea Vegetable Saute

Become acquainted with the delicious variety of sea vegetables available. Here, we combine the sweetness of carrots with the flavor of nori (a seaweed) and tamari.

Makes 4 servings

2 teaspoons sesame oil
3 carrots, thinly sliced diagonally
½ sheet nori (4 × 7 inches)
2 teaspoons tamari
1 tablespoon minced fresh parsley

Place the oil in a large skillet over medium heat. Add the carrots and stir. Turn heat to low and cover the pan.

Toast the nori over a stove burner. It will turn slightly brown and begin to curl. Do not allow it to burn.

Crumble the nori into the skillet with the carrots. Add the tamari. Steam, stirring frequently, over low heat until the carrots are firm-tender. Add a few drops of water, if necessary, to keep the vegetables from scorching.

Serve hot, garnished with parsley.

Vegetables Harvested from the Ocean Floor

Many people avoid sea vegetables (seaweeds) because they are so unlike the land vegetables they're accustomed to. But people living near the beach have been acquainted with the fine flavor and nutrition of sea vegetables for centuries. Seaweeds have a prominent place in the cuisines of the Far East, and they are also traditional in Hawaii, Ireland and Canada.

Nutritionally, seaweeds hit the jackpot. Although they do contain some sodium, they are also rich in calcium and phosphorus. They're a rich source of iodine, too—which is especially important if you have eliminated iodized salt from your diet. Magnesium, potassium, iron, copper and sulfur also are found in seaweeds. As for vitamins, one popular variety (nori) contains as much vitamin C, ounce for ounce, as do lemons, and more vitamin A than chicken livers. Seaweeds are also high in vitamins E, B_1 and B_{12}, as well as niacin, folate and pantothenate. Seaweeds are good for you. And the taste? Well, we won't spoil the surprise. Try the Carrot and Sea Vegetable Saute on this page, and you'll discover a centuries-old secret of the dwellers by the sea.

Ways with Brown Rice

Brown rice is a staple of natural foods cookery. This whole grain retains both its valuable bran layer and its germ, giving it a hands-down nutritional lead over polished white rice. You can choose short-grain or long-grain brown rice, depending on how it will be used. Short-grain rice has a nuttier flavor, sticks together and is better for casseroles and puddings. Choose long-grain rice for pilafs and other mixtures where the grains must be fluffy.

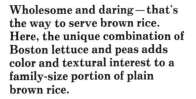

Wholesome and daring—that's the way to serve brown rice. Here, the unique combination of Boston lettuce and peas adds color and textural interest to a family-size portion of plain brown rice.

Pecan and Wild Rice Pilaf ● ●

Makes 6 servings

¾ cup uncooked brown rice
¼ cup uncooked wild rice
2 cups Garden-Vegetable Chicken Stock (page 53)
1 small onion, peeled
1 whole clove
2 tablespoons finely grated carrots
1 shallot, finely minced
1 cup pecan halves
1 tablespoon Butter-Half (page 133)

Place the rices, stock, the onion, stuck with the clove, the carrots and shallots in a medium saucepan. Bring to a boil, then reduce heat as low as possible, cover and steam 50 minutes.

Remove from heat and keep covered. Melt the butter in a medium skillet and lightly brown the pecans.

Remove the onion and clove from the rice. Toss the rice, then stir in the pecans. Serve hot.

Brown Rice and Bulgur ● ●

Use as a basis for pilaf or serve in place of plain brown rice.

Makes 6 servings

1 cup uncooked brown rice
½ cup bulgur
3 cups Low-Sodium Chicken Stock (page 52) or water

Place the rice, bulgur and stock or water in a medium saucepan. Bring to a boil for 3 to 4 minutes.

Cover the pan and reduce heat as low as possible. Steam the rice and bulgur for about 40 minutes.

Turn off heat and allow the mixture to stand for another 5 to 10 minutes, covered. Fluff with a fork and serve, or cool, then store.

NOTE: For pilaf, saute chopped or shredded vegetables in oil, then stir in cooked grains and heat through. Season with tamari.

Saffron Brown Rice ●

Special color and special flavor for special times.

Makes 8 servings

4 cups Low-Sodium Chicken Stock
    (page 52)
1 onion, peeled
½ teaspoon saffron threads
⅛ teaspoon ground cinnamon
1 tablespoon butter
2 cups uncooked long-grain brown
    rice

Place the stock, onion, saffron and cinnamon in a large saucepan and bring to a boil. Reduce heat, cover and simmer for 20 minutes.

Remove the onion (it can be saved for later use in soup or stew), and bring the stock to a rolling boil.

Add the butter. When it has melted, slowly add the rice in a trickle, so that the stock continues to boil.

When all the rice has been added, reduce the heat as low as possible, cover tightly and steam for 40 to 45 minutes. Turn off the heat and allow it to stand another 5 to 10 minutes, covered. Fluff up the rice and serve.

Variation: To make *Saffron Brown Rice Pilaf,* cook 1 sweet Spanish onion, minced, slowly in 1 tablespoon sunflower oil and 2 tablespoons butter. When the onion is tender but not browned, stir in ¼ cup slivered almonds, ¼ cup chopped pitted dates and 2 tablespoons dried currants. An optional tablespoon of honey stirred into the mixture adds a sweet flavor to the pilaf. Fold the onion mixture into the hot, cooked saffron rice before serving.

Leek–Brown Rice Pilaf ●

The use of leeks makes this one of the most flavorful ways to serve brown rice as a side dish.

Makes 4 servings

1 cup finely chopped leeks
2 tablespoons sunflower oil
3 cups cooked brown rice
    tamari, to taste

Cook the leeks in the oil in a large skillet over medium heat, stirring often. When the leeks are tender, stir in the rice.

Continue to stir the leeks and rice together until the rice is heated through. Turn the rice and leeks out into a serving bowl. Sprinkle with tamari. Serve hot.

Variation: For *Sweet Onion Rice,* substitute 1¼ cup chopped sweet Spanish onions for the leeks.

Pecan and Wild Rice Pilaf is a full-bodied yet elegant company dish.

New-Age Beverages: Hot 'n' Cold

Enjoy the zip without the zap.
With no alcohol, no caffeine,
these contain good nutrition.

When it comes to beverages, most of us are in a deep rut. Stuck in the boring routine of coffee, cola and booze, we can't see the world of nutritious, delicious beverages around us.

For instance, on a hot summer day, instead of longing for those colas or coladas, try one of our juicy fruit drinks or fizzes. They're truly refreshing, and most are loaded with vitamin C and potassium—two nutrients that can help your body maintain its cool in hot weather. Moreover, you won't suffer alcoholic relapse—that moment when the zip wears off and you just feel zapped.

When it's cold, similar rules apply. In fact, alcoholic drinks can be dangerous if you're involved in outdoor sports. The alcohol increases blood flow near the skin, which can eventually leave you colder.

What to choose instead? Try a Thermos of Mulled Apple Punch on your next skiing outing. A combination of herb tea and apple juice or cider will warm you inside and out.

And for children, you can skip the hot chocolate. Many of the commercial varieties contain far too much sugar. Instead, sample our Hot 'n' Creamy Carob, which does not contain caffeine and theobromine, two powerful stimulants found in chocolate. Hot carob makes a rich-tasting, healthy beverage the kids will really enjoy.

For the holidays, serve Pomegranate Toddies, Strawberry Spritzers or Holiday Cranberry Mugs. Your guests will enjoy alternatives to overdoing it with alcohol.

These "new-age" beverages represent a fresh approach that utilizes exciting new ingredients. Kiwi, honeydew melons, pomegranates and watermelon are not the usual grape-lemon-cherry flavors. The resulting drinks provide a nice bit of excitement and elegance.

Pineapple-Mint Frappe ●●

Makes 1 serving

½ cup chopped pineapple
½ cup apple juice
2 ice cubes
1 teaspoon fresh mint leaves
    whole strawberry (garnish)
    pineapple wedge (garnish)
    mint sprig (garnish)

Place the pineapple, apple juice, ice and mint leaves in a blender. Process on medium speed until smooth and frothy.

Strain the mixture into a glass. Place the strawberry, pineapple wedge and mint sprig on a stirring stick or toothpick and set in the glass or across the rim.

Strawberry Spritzer ●●●

Makes 2 servings

½ cup sliced strawberries
½ cup orange juice
½ cup apple juice
½ cup sparkling mineral water
2 ice cubes
2 whole strawberries with caps
    (garnish)

Place the sliced strawberries, juices, mineral water and ice in a blender. Process on medium speed until smooth.

Serve in chilled glasses. Slit the whole strawberries from the tips halfway to the caps and slip one over the rim of each glass.

Fruited Apple Punch ●●●

Makes 8 servings

4 cups chilled apple juice
4 cups chilled sparkling mineral
        water
1 lemon
1 cup strawberries
1 apple, cored and thinly sliced
4 orange slices, halved
    mint sprigs (garnish)

Place the apple juice and mineral water in a punch bowl. Squeeze the lemon and add the juice to the punch.

Add the strawberries and apple and orange slices to the bowl. Garnish with mint sprigs.

NOTE: You can keep the punch cold by placing the punch bowl in a larger bowl of crushed ice.

Old-Fashioned Lemonade ● ●

Makes 1½ quarts

4 to 5 lemons
5 cups water
3 tablespoons honey
  lemon slices (garnish)
  mint sprigs (garnish)

Finely grate the rind of one lemon and set aside. Squeeze the lemons to obtain 1 cup of juice.

Place the lemon juice and rind, water and honey in a 2-quart container. Chill.

Stir or shake well before serving over ice in glasses garnished with lemon and mint.

Banana–Strawberry Shake ● ●

Makes 2 servings

1 small ripe banana, frozen
¾ cup milk
2 teaspoons maple syrup or honey
2 ripe strawberries, halved
¼ teaspoon vanilla extract
2 whole strawberries with caps
    (garnish)

Place the banana, milk, maple syrup or honey, strawberry halves and vanilla in a blender. Process on low to medium speed until smooth.

Place the blended drink in two chilled glasses. Slit the whole strawberries from the tips halfway to the caps and slip one over the rim of each glass. Serve immediately.

NOTE: To freeze bananas, peel, wrap in foil or plastic wrap and place in freezer.

Iced Watermelon Frappe ● ●

Makes 2 servings

2 cups seeded watermelon cubes
½ cup apple juice
2 teaspoons fresh lime juice
3 to 4 ice cubes
2 pineapple spears (garnish)
2 whole strawberries (garnish)

Place the watermelon, juices and ice in a blender. Process on medium speed until smooth.

Serve in two frosty-cold glasses. To garnish, insert a toothpick through each pineapple spear and strawberry and rest one across the edge of each glass.

Variation: Add some ripe strawberries to the mixture before blending, or use frozen strawberries and omit ice cubes.

Orange Punch ●

When you want a "coffee break" without caffeine, try this robust fruit drink.

Makes 1 serving

¾ cup orange juice
¼ cup milk
 1 egg yolk
 1 teaspoon honey
 2 drops vanilla extract
 2 ice cubes
   orange slice (garnish)
   mint sprig (garnish)

Place the orange juice, milk, egg yolk and honey in a blender. Process until smooth. (Be sure the honey is mixed in.) Add ice, then process again until ice is crushed.

Place the drink in a tall, frosty-cold glass. Garnish with an orange slice, cut just to the center and slipped over the rim of the glass. Add a mint sprig, too.

Frosted Honeydew Cup ● ●

Makes 2 servings

1 cup cubed ripe honeydew melon
1 cup white grape juice
2 mint leaves
1 drop lemon extract
2 whole strawberries with caps
   (garnish)

Place the melon cubes, grape juice, mint and lemon extract in a blender and process on low to medium speed until smooth.

To serve, pour blended mixture into chilled glasses filled with crushed ice. Slit the whole strawberries from the tips halfway to the caps and slip one over the rim of each glass.

Kiwi Cooler ● ●

Makes 2 servings

 4 ripe kiwi fruits
⅓ cup white grape juice or apple
   juice
 2 teaspoons honey
1½ cups sparkling mineral water
 2 lime slices (garnish)
 2 whole strawberries (garnish)
 2 mint sprigs (garnish)

Peel the kiwi fruits and cut into quarters. Place them in a blender with the grape or apple juice and the honey.

Process on low to medium speed until smooth. Place the mixture in a sieve and press through with a spoon to remove the seeds.

Place half of the kiwi pulp into each of two tall glasses with ice. Pour in the mineral water and stir until combined.

Thread a lime slice, a strawberry and a mint sprig on each of two toothpicks and balance one on the rim of each glass. Serve immediately.

144

Natural Fruit-Ade

When the kids come clamoring for something to drink, forget about those mixes loaded with sugar and propped up with artificial flavors and colors. Instead, give 'em a refresher that's all natural. Combine fruit juice with sparkling mineral water for a fizzy treat. Or mix apple juice half and half with water for an inexpensive drink that still tastes great to the mini-sneaker set. And to really knock them off their Keds, add berries to the ice cubes!

Hot Drinks

Melt winter's icy grip with a warming drink by the fireside. Cuddle up with some Mulled Apple Punch, a drink that combines cider with herb tea. Or try the rather exotic Pomegranate Toddy, Holiday Cranberry Mug—made with fresh cranberries—or a cup of Hot 'n' Creamy Carob—the friendly alternative to hot chocolate.

Mulled Apple Punch
● ● ●

Makes 1 serving

½ cup water
½ cup apple juice or cider
1 rosehips tea bag
1 cinnamon stick

Bring the water and apple juice or cider to a boil in a small saucepan. Place the tea bag in a mug and pour in the boiling liquid.

Add the cinnamon and steep 3 to 4 minutes. Remove the tea bag and serve.

Pomegranate Toddies
○ ● ●

Makes 2 servings

2 pomegranates
1½ cups water
1 teaspoon honey
1 cinnamon stick

Remove the seeds from the pomegranates. Place the seeds in a small saucepan with the water, honey and cinnamon.

Bring to a boil, then reduce heat, simmer 2 to 3 minutes and remove from heat. Remove the cinnamon stick. Pour the mixture through a double layer of cheesecloth into a small bowl. Allow to cool.

Carefully twist the cheesecloth into a bag and squeeze the juice from the seeds. Return the liquid to the saucepan and heat before serving.

Variation: Serve chilled, in glasses garnished with lemon slices.

Holiday Cranberry Mugs ●●●

Makes 4 servings

2 cups cranberries
2 cups apple juice
1 tablespoon honey
4 lemon slices
  dash of freshly grated nutmeg
4 cinnamon sticks (garnish)

Place the cranberries and apple juice in a large saucepan and bring to a boil. Reduce heat and simmer 5 minutes, until most of the cranberries have burst.

Line a colander with cheesecloth, place the colander in a large bowl, and pour in the cranberries and juice. Bring up the edges of the cheesecloth to form a bag and press the remaining juice from the cranberries with the back of a wooden spoon.

Return the mixture to the saucepan. Add the honey and lemon slices and bring just to the boiling point. Sprinkle with nutmeg.

Ladle the hot mixture into mugs and garnish with cinnamon sticks.

Hot 'n' Creamy Carob ●●

Makes 1 serving

1 cup milk
1 teaspoon maple syrup
1 tablespoon carob powder
1 drop vanilla extract

Heat the milk in a small saucepan until scalded (small bubbles will appear in the milk around the edge of the pan).

Place the syrup and carob in a mug. Add about 1 tablespoon of milk and stir until smooth.

Stir in remaining milk and add vanilla. Serve piping hot.

Variation: Substitute honey for the maple syrup.

13

Desserts without Guilt

For the special occasion, or just because *you're* special, enjoy these healthy desserts.

Children often prefer dessert over any other part of a meal—and it's a preference many of us never outgrow. Instead of feeling guilty, simply make desserts measure up to your nutritional standards. Prepared wisely, this course can complete the day's balance of essential nutrients. Moreover, healthful ingredients can be elegant enough for a special dinner or charming enough to send the nursery school set into wriggles of delight.

The healthiest dessert of all, of course, is fresh fruit. But don't think only in terms of a bowl filled with apples and pears. Instead, think about fruit with *pizzazz*. Think Watermelon Fruit Bowl.

The watermelon, hollowed out, will be your serving dish, handsome enough for a centerpiece. Balls of watermelon and cantaloupe, cubed pineapple, apples and whole grapes create the colorful combination spooned inside.

And think Jeweled Fresh Fruit Torte and Sunflower-Apricot Cookies. All these cakes and cookies rely on whole grains and carob, nuts and fruit to add a variety of nutrients and fiber to your diet. For a "company" dessert, try the rich Dark Forest Carob Torte, shown opposite. You've never tasted carob prepared so deliciously. Though you won't want to serve the richest of these desserts too often, when you do, the calories you consume will do you some good.

Be sure to check out the variety of cookies— old favorites like Oatmeal Raisin and Brown-Edge Wafers are challenged by daring new cookies such as Black Walnut-Caraway Tea Cookies and others made with sunflower seeds and dried apricots. They're fun, fiber-filled and delicious.

Dark Forest Carob Torte ● ●

A deep fruity flavor complements the carob in this moist, layered confection.

Makes 10 servings

Cake
½ cup carob powder, sifted
¼ cup corn oil
½ cup maple syrup
1 egg
2 teaspoons grated orange rind
1 teaspoon vanilla extract
¼ teaspoon almond extract
½ cup buttermilk
1½ cups unbleached flour
1 teaspoon baking soda
½ teaspoon ground cinnamon
⅛ teaspoon ground allspice
⅛ teaspoon ground cloves
Filling
¼ cup dried apricots
¾ cup water
1 tablespoon orange juice
¼ teaspoon grated orange rind
Icing
3 tablespoons butter
3 tablespoons maple syrup
1 tablespoon light unsulfured
    molasses
1 tablespoon orange juice or milk
¼ cup carob powder, sifted

To make the cake, place the carob, oil and maple syrup in a large bowl and stir together until smooth. Beat in the egg, then the orange rind and vanilla and almond extracts. Stir in the buttermilk until the mixture is smooth.

In a smaller bowl, combine the flour, baking soda, cinnamon, allspice and cloves. Add the dry ingredients to the wet ingredients and stir just until smoothly combined.

Spread the batter evenly in a buttered and floured or lightly oiled 8-inch round cake pan. Bake in a preheated 350°F oven for 25 to 30 minutes, or just until a knife inserted in the center comes out clean. Do not overbake, or the cake will be dry.

While the cake is baking, prepare the filling. Combine the apricots and water in a small saucepan. Bring to a boil over medium heat, then reduce heat to low, cover tightly and simmer about 30 minutes, or just until the apricots are plump and the liquid is absorbed.

Place the apricots with the orange juice and orange rind in a blender. Process on low to medium speed until smooth, stopping to stir the mixture, if necessary, so that all the apricots are well blended.

When the cake has finished baking, allow it to cool for a minute or two, until it shrinks back from the sides of the pan. Then invert the cake on a cake rack to cool.

When the cake has cooled, remove it from the pan. Using a long, serrated knife, cut the cake in half horizontally. Remove the upper round of cake and invert it on another cake rack. Spread this half with apricot filling.

Place the other half of the cake right side up over the filling.

To prepare the icing, melt the butter in a small saucepan. Stir in the maple syrup and molasses, the orange juice or milk and the carob.

Spread the icing over the cake, allowing it to drip down the sides. When the cake is iced, place it on a serving plate. Serve at room temperature, or chill.

NOTE: In season, fresh flowers are a most attractive garnish for this dark cake. Use violet flowers and leaves, or petals from pansies, roses, apple blossoms or carnations. All of these flowers are edible, but if you do plan to eat them, be certain that they are pesticide free.

Fruit Kabobs ● ● ●

Makes 4 servings

¼ ripe pineapple
2 kiwi fruits
2 nectarines
12 large ripe strawberries

Peel the pineapple and remove the tough inner fibers. Cut into 12 pieces.

Peel the kiwi fruits and cut each into six wedges.

Remove the pits from the nectarines and cut each into six wedges.

Arrange the fruit on skewers, alternating the pineapple, kiwi wedges, nectarine wedges and strawberries. Place on a large platter of crushed ice.

Maple Whipped Cream ● ●

Makes 2 cups

1 cup heavy cream
2 teaspoons maple syrup
¼ teaspoon vanilla extract

Chill the beaters and mixing bowl before whipping the cream.

Using an electric mixer on low speed, or whisking by hand, beat the cream until it begins to thicken.

Add the maple syrup and vanilla. Continue to beat, on medium speed if using a mixer, until the whipped cream forms soft peaks when the beaters or whisk are removed. Store tightly covered in the refrigerator.

Crepes with Apple-Cinnamon Filling ●

Makes 2 servings

1 large tart apple
1 tablespoon butter
3 tablespoons apple juice or cider
1 teaspoon maple syrup
  dash of ground cinnamon
4 crepes
  Maple Whipped Cream (this page)

Peel and thinly slice the apple. (Use a firm baking-type apple, such as Granny Smith.)

Melt the butter in a medium skillet. Add the apple slices and cook, stirring often, over medium heat.

As the apples cook, add some apple juice or cider, a tablespoon at a time, and continue to stir until the apples are tender. Stir in the maple syrup and cinnamon.

Divide the filling among the crepes, and either roll the filling in the crepes or fold the crepes in half over the apples. Top with whipped cream and serve.

Meringue Pie Shell ● ● ●

Prepare this pie shell well before you intend to serve it.

Makes 1 9-inch pie shell

5 egg whites
¼ teaspoon cream of tartar
¼ cup honey

Beat the egg whites with the cream of tartar until they form stiff peaks.

Add the honey and continue to beat until it is thoroughly incorporated into the egg whites.

Pour the egg whites into a buttered 9-inch pie plate. Spoon out the center of the whites, leaving a thin layer on the bottom of the pie plate, and add the extra meringue in peaks around the outside of the meringue shell.

Place the pie shell in a preheated 400°F oven and turn off the oven immediately. Let the pie shell rest, undisturbed, for 1½ hours.

Fill the pie shell with fresh fruit or other filling.

151

Apple-Pecan Cheese Torte ● ●

Makes 10 servings

Crust
⅓ cup whole wheat flour
⅓ cup unbleached flour
2 tablespoons brown rice flour
¼ cup cold butter
1 egg yolk
2 teaspoons honey
2 drops vanilla extract
2 to 3 teaspoons water
Filling
½ pound cream cheese
⅓ cup cottage cheese
¼ cup yogurt
¼ cup maple syrup
2 eggs
½ teaspoon vanilla extract
Topping
4 cups peeled sliced apples
¼ cup honey
½ teaspoon ground cinnamon
⅓ cup chopped pecans
1 tablespoon butter

To make the crust, place the flours in a food processor or a large bowl. Cut in the butter with several quick on-and-off turns of the processor, fitted with the steel blade, or by hand with a pastry blender.

With several turns of the food processor or with a fork, blend in the egg yolk, honey, vanilla and enough water to make the crumbly mixture hold together.

Press the dough into the bottom of and about ¾ inch up the sides of a buttered and floured 8-inch springform pan.

To prepare the filling, blend together the cheeses, yogurt, maple syrup, eggs and vanilla on medium speed in a blender, or in a food processor fitted with the steel blade, until smooth.

Prepare the topping by gently tossing together the apples, honey and cinnamon in a large bowl until the apples are coated. Reserve any liquid.

Bake the torte crust for 5 minutes in a preheated 350°F oven. Pour the cheese mixture into the crust.

Overlap whole apple slices around the outside of the cheesecake. (There will be about two layers of slices.) Put any broken pieces of apple slices into the center. Sprinkle the top with pecans.

Melt the butter in a small saucepan. Add liquid from the apples left in the large bowl. Cook over medium heat until most of the liquid has evaporated and the mixture is thick and bubbly. Spoon evenly over the torte.

Bake at 350°F for 1 hour. Allow to cool, then run a knife around the outside of the cheesecake and remove the ring collar from the pan. Cover with plastic wrap or foil and chill.

Variations: Substitute honey for maple syrup. Reduce cottage cheese to ¼ cup and substitute sour cream for yogurt.

Marbled Souffle Cheesecake ● ● ●

Makes 10 to 12 servings

Crust
1 cup rolled oats
⅓ cup whole wheat flour
¼ cup ground almonds
3 tablespoons safflower oil
1 to 2 tablespoons apple juice
Filling
1½ pounds tofu
¾ cup maple syrup
3 eggs, separated
3 tablespoons lemon juice
1 teaspoon grated lemon rind
2 tablespoons arrowroot
2 teaspoons vanilla extract
⅓ cup carob powder
Topping
1 kiwi fruit
1 pint strawberries
½ cup blueberries
1 nectarine

To prepare the crust, combine the oats, flour, almonds, oil and enough apple juice to bind the ingredients in a medium bowl.

Press the crust into the bottom of an oiled 8-inch springform pan. Bake in a preheated 375°F oven for 15 minutes. Remove from the oven.

The secret ingredient in this elegant, marbled cheesecake is tofu, thus making it a healthful high-flavor dessert.

To make the filling, bring a large pot of water, three-fourths full, to a boil over high heat. Cut the tofu into large pieces and gently drop them into the boiling water. Simmer 1 minute, then remove with a slotted spoon.

Place the tofu, syrup, egg yolks, lemon juice and rind, arrowroot and vanilla in a food processor fitted with the steel blade. Process until smooth. If using a blender, crumble the tofu and blend half of the mixture at a time, stopping to scrape down the sides as necessary.

Place half of the processed or blended mixture in a medium bowl.

Add the carob to the tofu mixture remaining in the processor or blender. Process until combined.

Beat the egg whites until they form stiff peaks. Place the carob mixture in a medium bowl. Fold half the egg whites into the carob-tofu mixture and half into the plain tofu mixture.

Using a large spoon, alternate dollops of plain and carob filling in the springform pan. Bake in a preheated 375°F oven for 30 to 40 minutes, until the filling is firm.

Turn off the oven and leave the cheesecake in with the door slightly ajar. Remove after 30 minutes. Run a wet knife around the edge of the cheesecake to remove the ring collar. When the cheesecake is cool, decorate the top with alternating rings of sliced fresh fruit.

Maple Yogurt Sauce
● ● ●

Makes ½ cup

½ cup yogurt
 1 tablespoon maple syrup
¼ teaspoon vanilla extract

In a small bowl, stir the ingredients together until well blended.
    Store tightly covered in the refrigerator.

Banana Layer Cake

Makes 3 8-inch layers

This may be dessert, but there's not an empty calorie in sight. The banana cake is layered and filled with Apple-Prune Butter, the top decorated with almonds.

 ¾ cup butter
 ⅓ cup corn oil
1⅓ cups honey
1½ cups buttermilk
 2 ripe bananas
 3 eggs

1½ teaspoons vanilla extract
2¼ cups whole wheat flour
 1 cup unbleached flour
1½ teaspoons baking soda
 ¾ teaspoon baking powder
 ½ cup Apple-Prune Butter (page 20)
   slivered almonds (garnish)

Place the butter in a small saucepan over low heat. When the butter has melted, stir in the oil and honey.
    Place the buttermilk, bananas, eggs and vanilla in a blender and process on medium speed until smooth.
    In a large bowl, combine the flours, baking soda and baking powder. Add the butter mixture and the banana mixture and stir just until combined.
    Divide the batter among three oiled 8-inch cake pans. Bake in a preheated 350°F oven for about 25 minutes, or until a cake tester inserted in the center comes out clean.
    Turn the layers out on wire racks and allow to cool slightly before proceeding. While the cake is still warm, place one layer on a serving plate and spread it with ¼ cup of apple-prune butter. Place the second layer on top and spread with the remaining apple-prune butter. Add the final layer, then dust the top of the cake with ground almonds.

Variation: Substitute any other favorite fruit spread for the apple-prune butter.

Orange-Raisin-Date Bars ●

Makes 16 bars

½ cup safflower oil
1 egg
1 teaspoon vanilla extract
1 teaspoon grated orange rind
1 cup chopped dates
¼ cup raisins
1 cup rolled oats
1 cup whole wheat flour
1 teaspoon baking powder
1 teaspoon ground cinnamon
¼ teaspoon ground allspice
½ cup sunflower seeds
⅔ cup orange juice

In a large bowl, combine the oil, egg, vanilla, orange rind, dates and raisins. Stir together well.

In a medium bowl, combine the oats, flour, baking powder, cinnamon, allspice and sunflower seeds.

Add the dry ingredients to the wet ingredients and stir in the orange juice.

Spread the batter in a lightly oiled, shallow 9 × 13-inch baking pan. Bake in a preheated 350°F oven for 20 to 25 minutes. Cut into 16 bars.

Sorbet

Using a blender or food processor, you can turn a few frozen strawberries and a little whipped cream into a smooth-as-silk sorbet. You'll need 1 cup of whole frozen berries. Place them in either a processor or blender, along with 2 tablespoons maple syrup. Process until smooth, stopping to scrape down the inside of the container with a spatula as necessary. If you're working with a food processor, add ¼ cup whipped cream and process the mixture just until it has been combined. If you're working with a blender, remove the blended strawberry mixture to a small bowl and quickly fold in the whipped cream with a spatula. Spoon sorbet into a chilled serving dish and place it in the freezer for a few minutes, if necessary, to firm it before serving.

Country Applesauce Squares with Currants ●

Makes 16 squares

¼ cup sunflower oil
¼ cup butter
¼ cup honey
1 cup applesauce
1 egg, beaten
½ teaspoon vanilla extract
½ cup currants
1 cup whole wheat flour
½ cup bran
1 teaspoon baking powder
1 teaspoon ground cinnamon
⅛ teaspoon ground cloves
⅛ teaspoon ground allspice
   dash of ground nutmeg
½ cup walnuts

Place the oil, butter and honey in a small saucepan over low heat. When the butter has melted, stir in the applesauce, eggs, vanilla and currants.

In a medium bowl, combine the flour, bran, baking powder and spices.

Stir the wet ingredients into the dry ingredients just until combined.

Place the batter in a lightly oiled 8-inch square baking pan. Press the walnuts into the top of the batter. Bake in a preheated 325°F oven for 45 minutes, or until golden.

Cool, then cut into squares.

Variation: Eliminate butter and use ½ cup sunflower oil.

The Crown jewels couldn't look more elegant than the fresh fruit combination topping this torte. Choose any colorful assortment of fruits, depending on the season.

Jeweled Fresh Fruit Torte ● ●

Makes 12 servings

Crust
1¾ cup unbleached flour
¼ cup whole wheat pastry flour
1 teaspoon baking powder
½ cup plus 3 tablespoons cold butter
3 egg yolks
1 teaspoon vanilla extract
¼ cup honey
2 tablespoons cold water
¼ cup dry whole wheat bread crumbs
Glaze
½ cup apple juice or white grape juice
½ cup cold water
1 tablespoon cornstarch
1 tablespoon honey
Winter Topping
24 to 36 seedless grapes
1 to 2 bananas
2 oranges
Summer Topping
1 cup strawberries
2 to 3 kiwi fruits
½ cup finely chopped pineapple
Garnish (optional)
Maple Whipped Cream
(page 151)

To make the crust, combine the flours and the baking powder in a large bowl or in a food processor fitted with the steel blade, using a few quick on-and-off turns.

Cut the butter into the flour with a pastry knife or with quick on-and-off turns of the processor, just until the mixture looks sandy.

Add the egg yolks, vanilla, honey and water and mix together lightly with a fork, or in the food processor for about 15 seconds, until you can shape smooth dough.

Flatten the dough slightly and chill, tightly wrapped in plastic wrap, for 30 minutes. Place the bread crumbs in a well-buttered German torte pan and shake until the bottom and sides are coated.

Roll out the dough between two pieces of waxed paper until it spreads to about ¾ inch larger than the outside diameter of the torte pan. Use the bottom piece of waxed paper to place the dough into the pan. Gently press dough into the recessed outer rim of the pan. Lightly prick the dough with a fork.

Bake in a preheated 325°F oven for about 25 minutes, or until it is golden brown and lightly puffed.

Allow the crust to cool well. Place a large cake platter over the pan and invert the pan. Rap the bottom of the pan to release the crust.

To prepare the glaze, place the ingredients in a small saucepan. Stir until the cornstarch is dissolved.

Over low to medium heat, stir the mixture until it becomes clear and begins to thicken. Set aside to cool slightly.

To arrange the winter topping on the torte shell, begin with a single line of grapes, halved or whole, around the edge. Slice the bananas on the diagonal and overlap slightly, forming another ring just inside the grapes.

Peel the oranges. Remove the membranes from the orange sections and arrange the sections in another, smaller circle. Add another circle of banana slices and a grape in the center.

For the summer topping, halve the strawberries and arrange on the outer perimeter of the torte. Add slices of kiwi fruit, slightly overlapped, just inside the ring of berries. Add a thin circle of chopped pineapple, then additional berries or kiwi fruit. Fill in any gaps, if desired, with chopped pineapple.

Spoon the glaze evenly over the fruit. (If it becomes too stiff from cooling, reheat briefly.) If desired, chill before serving, and garnish with whipped cream.

Variation: Use any soft, colorful fruit to decorate torte, including blueberries, raspberries, peaches, papaya.

Watermelon Fruit Bowl ● ● ●

Makes 8 to 10 servings

1 large round watermelon
1 small cantaloupe
¼ pineapple
2 apples
1 cup seedless grapes
    mint sprigs (garnish)

Cut the watermelon horizontally, removing one-third. Reserve this "top" for another use. With a melon

baller, remove as much of the flesh as possible from the melon. Remove any remaining flesh with a knife. Return the watermelon balls on the scooped-out melon shell.

Halve the cantaloupe and remove the seeds. Using the melon baller, scoop out the cantaloupe and add to the watermelon balls. Add any juice from the cantaloupe.

Peel and core the pineapple, then cube it. Add it, along with any juice, to the melon balls.

Quarter and core the apples. Cube and add to the watermelon shell. Add grapes and toss everything together.

Chill, then serve garnished with mint sprigs. Set in a bowl, if necessary, to make the watermelon stable.

NOTE: To make the watermelon even more attractive for serving, cut a decorative edge as you cut the top from the melon. Make short cuts at 90-degree angles for a sawtooth effect.

Give them your best! The most healthful dessert, fresh fruit, is served up here in sweet abundance.

Carob–Maple Dessert Topping ● ●

Skip the artificial dessert toppings: Satisfy your craving with a calcium-rich whip that's all natural!

Makes 1 cup

1 cup part-skim ricotta cheese
2 tablespoons maple syrup
1 tablespoon sifted carob powder
¼ teaspoon vanilla extract

Place the cheese in a blender. Stir together the remaining ingredients and add to blender.

Process on low speed, stopping to scrape down the sides once or twice. Blend until the mixture is smooth and creamy.

Use as a dessert topping, or spread over crepes, roll up and top with chopped fresh fruit.

Refrigerate unused portion tightly covered.

Carob–Nut Squares

Carob and walnuts combine for flavorful dessert squares. To make them extra-special, top them with whipped cream.

Makes 9 squares

Chocolatey-good, but sensibly carob. From top: Carob-Date Souffle, Carob-Nut Squares, Carob-Maple Dessert Topping and Cinnamon-Carob Crepes.

½ cup whole wheat pastry flour
¼ cup brown rice flour
½ cup carob powder
½ teaspoon baking powder
½ cup peanut butter
½ cup honey
¼ cup butter, melted
3 eggs
1 egg white
½ teaspoon vanilla extract
1 cup chopped walnuts
9 walnut halves (garnish)

In a large bowl, combine the flours, carob and baking powder.

In a medium bowl, combine the peanut butter, honey, butter, eggs, egg white and vanilla.

Stir the wet ingredients into the dry ingredients, along with the chopped walnuts, just until the mixture is smooth.

Spread the batter in a lightly oiled 8-inch square baking dish. Arrange the walnut halves in three rows of three across the top of the batter.

Bake in a preheated 350°F oven for 25 minutes, or until a cake tester inserted in the center comes out clean. Allow to cool and cut into 9 squares.

Carob-Date Souffle
● ● ●

An elegant cold-weather dessert.

Makes 6 servings

1 cup pitted dates
¾ cup milk
4 eggs
2 tablespoons maple syrup
2 tablespoons carob powder, sifted
1 teaspoon vanilla extract
½ teaspoon grated orange rind
⅛ teaspoon almond extract

Place the dates and milk in a small saucepan over medium heat. Bring to a boil, then reduce heat, cover and simmer until the dates are well softened, about 10 minutes. Set aside to cool.

Separate the eggs, placing the whites in a medium bowl and the yolks in a blender. Add the maple syrup, carob, vanilla, orange rind and almond extract to the egg yolks.

Place the dates and milk in the blender with the carob mixture and process on low speed until smooth, stopping to scrape down the sides as necessary.

Place the blended mixture in a large bowl. By hand or with an electric mixer first on low, then on medium speed, beat the egg whites until they form stiff peaks.

Fold about one-fourth of the egg whites into the carob mixture to lighten it. Then gently fold in the remaining egg whites with a spatula. Pour into a buttered medium souffle dish.

Bake in a preheated 350°F oven for 35 to 40 minutes, or until the souffle is puffed and golden brown. Serve immediately.

Cinnamon-Carob Crepes ● ●

Makes 16 crepes

1¼ cups skim milk
¼ cup sunflower oil
3 tablespoons apple juice
1 tablespoon honey
¼ teaspoon vanilla extract
3 eggs
½ cup whole wheat pastry flour
¼ cup unbleached flour
¼ cup carob powder
½ teaspoon ground cinnamon

Place the milk, oil, juice, honey, vanilla and eggs in a blender. Process on low speed until combined.

Add the flours, carob and cinnamon. Process on low to medium speed until smooth, stopping to scrape down the sides once or twice.

Pour a few tablespoons of the batter into a crepe pan and swirl to coat the bottom of the pan. Cook over medium-high heat until the surface of the crepe appears dry.

Slide the crepe out of the pan onto a kitchen towel draped over cake racks, and allow the crepe to cool before handling. Repeat with remaining batter.

Carob—The All-Around Winner

Carob tastes somewhat like chocolate and cocoa, but has several advantages over them. Unlike cocoa, carob is naturally sweet, so there's no need to add a lot of sugar. It's also low in fat. And it's high in fiber, so it can play a modest role in reducing diets.

Carob has about 4 times the calcium of chocolate or cocoa and none of the oxalic acid, which binds calcium and prevents its absorption. Carob also is free of caffeine and theobromine, a stimulant related to caffeine that is also found in chocolate. Carob also has the added benefit of causing fewer allergic reactions than either cocoa or chocolate. Carob, it seems, is an all-around winner!

Cookies

Black Walnut–Caraway Tea Cookies ●

These sophisticated cookies aren't extra sweet.

Makes 2½ dozen

   2 eggs
   ⅓ cup honey
   ⅓ cup butter, melted
   1 teaspoon vanilla extract
   ½ teaspoon lemon extract
   ¼ teaspoon almond extract
   1¾ cups whole wheat flour
   ½ cup unbleached flour
   2 tablespoons brown rice flour
   2 teaspoons baking powder
   ½ teaspoon caraway seeds
   ¾ cup finely chopped black
      walnuts
      black walnut or pecan halves
      (garnish)

In a large bowl, beat the eggs. Beat in the honey and then the melted butter, cooled slightly. Add the vanilla, lemon and almond extracts.
   In a medium bowl, combine the flours, baking powder and caraway seeds. Stir the dry ingredients into the egg mixture, along with the walnuts.
   Lightly oil a tablespoon measure. Press the dough, a tablespoon at a time, into the measure to form a rounded cookie. Gently remove and place, rounded side up, on a lightly oiled baking sheet.
   Press black walnut or pecan halves into the tops of the cookies. Bake in a preheated 325°F oven for 20 minutes, or until the cookies are a light golden brown.

Brown-Edge Wafers ●

Makes 2½ dozen

   ½ cup unsalted butter, at room
      temperature
   ½ cup honey
   1 cup whole wheat pastry flour
   ½ cup brown rice flour
   1 egg, beaten
   ½ teaspoon vanilla extract

In a medium bowl, cream the butter with the honey, using a wooden spoon.
   Add the flours, egg and vanilla and stir just until the dough is smooth.
   Place the dough on a lightly oiled baking sheet, using about 2 teaspoons of dough for each cookie. Flatten the dough with the back of the spoon. Leave room for the cookies to spread.
   Bake in a preheated 350°F oven for 10 minutes, or until the cookies are flat, the edges are brown and the centers golden. Cool on wire racks. Store, tightly covered, in a cool, dry place.

Oatmeal-Raisin Cookies ●

Makes 2 to 2½ dozen

   ½ cup butter
   ½ cup honey or maple syrup
   1 egg, beaten
   1 tablespoon buttermilk
   1 teaspoon vanilla extract
   1 cup whole wheat flour
   ¼ cup brown rice flour
   ½ teaspoon baking soda
   ¼ teaspoon baking powder
   ⅛ teaspoon ground coriander
   1 cup rolled oats
   ½ cup raisins

Melt the butter in a small saucepan over low heat. Stir in the honey or maple syrup, and when the mixture has cooled slightly, stir in the egg, buttermilk and vanilla.

In a medium bowl, combine the flours, baking soda, baking powder, coriander, oats and raisins.

Stir the wet ingredients into the dry ingredients just until combined. Drop the cookies by the spoonful onto a lightly oiled baking sheet, leaving enough room for the cookies to spread.

Bake in a preheated 350°F oven for about 12 minutes, or until golden brown.

Nutty Walnut Drops
● ●

Makes 3 dozen

⅓ cup butter
⅓ cup maple syrup
½ teaspoon vanilla extract
¼ teaspoon finely grated lemon
    rind
1 cup whole wheat flour
2 tablespoons wheat germ
2 cups chopped walnuts
1 tablespoon buttermilk
½ teaspoon baking soda

Place the butter and maple syrup in a small saucepan over low heat. Warm just until the butter melts, then remove from heat. Stir in the vanilla and lemon rind.

In a medium bowl, combine the flour, wheat germ and walnuts.

Place the buttermilk in a cup and add the baking soda. Stir until dissolved.

Add the butter and maple syrup mixture along with the buttermilk to the dry ingredients. Stir just until combined.

Drop the batter by the teaspoon onto lightly oiled baking sheets. Bake in a preheated 325°F oven for 12 to 15 minutes, or until light golden brown. Cool on wire racks and store in a tightly covered container.

Sunflower-Apricot Cookies ●

Makes 2 to 2½ dozen

1 cup rolled oats
½ cup sunflower seeds
½ cup whole wheat flour
½ cup unbleached flour
1 teaspoon baking powder
½ teaspoon ground cinnamon
½ cup sunflower oil
½ cup honey
1 egg
1 teaspoon vanilla extract
½ cup finely chopped dried
    apricots

Place the oats in a medium bowl. Place the sunflower seeds in a blender and grind with short bursts at high speed.

Add the ground seeds, flours, baking powder and cinnamon to the oats and stir until combined.

Combine the oil, honey, egg, milk and vanilla in a small bowl. Add with the apricots to the dry ingredients and stir just until combined. Chill 3 to 4 hours, or overnight.

Drop the dough onto a lightly oiled baking sheet. Leave room for the cookies to spread. Bake in a preheated 350°F oven about 12 minutes, or until the cookies are golden brown. Remove to a rack to cool.

Our favorite cookies, from left: Black Walnut-Caraway Tea Cookies, Brown-Edge Wafers, Oatmeal-Raisin Cookies, Nutty Walnut Drops and Sunflower-Apricot Cookies.

Photography Credits

Staff Photographers—
Angelo M. Caggiano: pp. 42; 48-49; 50-51; 65, top right. Carl Doney: pp. 8; 29, top left; 32-33; 58-59; 70-71; 73; 74; 76-77; 78-79; 100-101; 105; 117; 128-129; 135; 140-141; 146-147; 157; 160-161. T. L. Gettings: p. 28, top right. John P. Hamel: pp. 17; 28, top left; 69. Mitchell T. Mandel: pp. 22-23; 31; 34-35; 40-41; 43, bottom; 56; 80; 103; 112-113; 136. Alison Miksch: pp. 3; 54; 55; 124; 131. Pat Seip: p. 29, top right. Margaret Skrovanek: pp. 1; 6-7; 14-15; 16; 18-19; 20-21; 26-27; 36; 43, top; 45; 64-65; 81; 86-87; 122-123. Christie C. Tito: p. 130. Sally Shenk Ullman: pp. 11; 12; 52-53; 60; 66-67; 88-89; 93; 94-95; 98-99; 106-107; 109; 115; 126-127; 138; 139; 142-143; 144; 145; 148-149; 153; 154; 156; 158.

*Additional Photos Courtesy of—*Freelance Photographers' Guild, New York, G. Schwartz: pp. 110-111.

Food Styling Credits

Ilene Allen: pp. 126-127. Barbara Fritz: pp. 11; 12; 18-19; 20-21; 36; 43, bottom; 50-51; 65, top right; 80; 86-87; 93; 112-113; 135; 146-147; 148-149; 153; 158. Kay Seng Lichthardt: pp. 6-7; 14-15; 16; 42; 43, top; 45; 69; 70-71; 76-77; 78-79; 81; 100-101; 106-107; 117; 122-123; 136; 140-141; 160-161. Laura Hendry Reifsnyder: pp. 17; 22-23; 26-27; 31; 32-33; 34-35; 40-41; 58-59; 64-65; 66-67; 73; 94-95; 98-99; 103; 109; 115; 128-129; 130; 138; 139; 142-143; 144; 154; 156; 157. Kathryn Sommons: pp. 60; 74; 88-89. Elinor Wilson: pp. 8; 56; 105; 131.

Illustration Credits

Bascove: p. 25, top and bottom. Susan Blubaugh: pp. 2; 4; 13; 25, center; 47; 61; 75; 91; 118; 119; 121; 125. Anita Lovitt: pp. 9; 30; 83; 90; 97; 104; 155. Donna Ruff: pp. 37; 57; 111; 132; 137; 159.

*Special Thanks to—*Jack Brewer, North Carolina; A Gift from Cherylz', Allentown, Pa.; Glose Stained Glass, Allentown, Pa.; Marion Grebow Fine Porcelain Dinnerware, Norwalk, Connecticut; Mr. & Mrs. Alexander Hendry; Mr. & Mrs. Edward Hyland; Dr. & Mrs. J. William Miksch; Dina Porter—The Gallery for Fine Gifts, Allentown, Pa.; Ritter's Furniture, Emmaus, Pa.; C. Leslie Smith, Silversmith, Allentown, Pa.; Terra Firma, New York; Valkris Pottery, Allentown, Pa.; WST Porcelain, New York.

Index